MW00980647

8

FIVEFOLD APOSTLE CHURCH BUILDING

Reformation, Restoring The New Testament Church

Apostle John DeVries

 FriesenPress

Suite 300 - 990 Fort St
Victoria, BC, V8V 3K2
Canada

www.friesenpress.com

All scriptures are from King James Authorized Version.
When texts are abbreviated the usage of ---- indicates this.
Some texts have been altered to modern English (thou –you)

Cover art: Bruce Abbot, Post Falls ID, USA

Editing by Sherrie Jenicek

ISBN
978-1-5255-1991-8 (Hardcover)
978-1-5255-1992-5 (Paperback)
978-1-5255-1993-2 (eBook)

1. RELIGION, CHRISTIAN CHURCH, GROWTH

Distributed to the trade by The Ingram Book Company

Printed in Canada

CONTENTS

ACKNOWLEDGEMENTS

It will not be enough to express our limited thanks, but we will have all of eternity to praise and worship our creator God of salvation for Christ, the cross, and our redemption. That is the greatest of all blessings to those who find salvation here, now, and forever.

The second greatest blessings in life are the believers who encourage us in our faith. They stabilize us in our faith walk, which is worth far more than gold.

I especially want to thank my prophetess wife, Siony, who supports me in writing. I thank God for our long-term pastoral "Timothy couple," Jamie and Sherrie Jenicek. They as Timothy who followed Paul are mature, having faithfully followed us in ministry. Their loving encouragement and support in our Post Falls ministry and lives have been invaluable. I thank my Canadian family, both natural and in the faith, who all encourage us in different ways. I thank Richard and Jo-Anne Blanchard; and Dr. Kevin and Barbara Orieux, who the Lord brought into our lives in a most unusual way. Their ministry mindedness has prospered the proliferation of thousands of doctrinal manuals.

I thank Apostle Reginald and Linda Holiday of Bethany Fellowship in North Carolina. While ministering there at a conference, Apostle Reginald asked, "How do we really build a fivefold church?" Praise God for this humble, transparent question from a fellow apostle. The Lord used this and immediately triggered a desire in me to respond to this question through the creation of this book.

I also want to acknowledge and thank the Lord for my faithful covenant fellow, Apostle Ernesto Balili, from Mindanao, Philippines. Throughout the years, we've shared a complete unity of understanding in fivefold truths as we have labored to build up a great many ministries and churches. Thank you, Lord Jesus, for the immeasurable privilege of being called to the ministry!

FOREWORD

I have studied the new book, "Fivefold Apostle Church Building," written by my ministry partner and co-apostle, John DeVries. This book contains the needed truths that will revolutionize the church for sincere Bible truth seekers. This book details the priorities in building "fivefold churches": churches in accordance to the God-given pattern and blueprint.

Unlike any book I have found, this writing sets out the strong need to seek out and keep God's ordinances, laws, government, and doctrines in our church building. I highly recommend this to all fivefold ministers and elders. All true ministries and disciples of our Lord Jesus Christ should have a copy of this powerful and eye-opening book. This will unleash them with knowledge and understanding in the realm of genuine fivefold revelational truths and knowledge.

I strongly encourage the reader to acquire copies of other books by Apostle John DeVries. His writings set out revelation knowledge of the apostles' Bible doctrines. This will help any reader and church *grow in the grace and knowledge of our Lord Jesus Christ*" (2 Pet. 1:2). His writings detail the needed topics of maturing the saints by a Christ-orchestrated government. We must return to a multiple eldership and ministry church. The Book of Acts and New Testament churches we read about must again be experienced. These will function again under God's restored apostles of today, along with prophets and all the Christ-given ministry callings and government.

For Kingdom expansion and extension,
—Apostle Ernie M. Balili

PREFACE

Existing global political turmoil and wars are not the most important topics affecting our lives; Christ's church, holy believers, the saints who belong to Jesus Christ, and having life eternal are many times more important. Heaven and earth will pass away, but Christ's Words never will.

The true believer is the precious fruit of the earth who waits for the soon-coming end-time's seventh trumpet, which will herald the resurrection of the dead.

The painful truth is that few are ready who joyfully look for His coming. The church is much divided throughout the earth, and it is now seen with many differing faces. The Bible New Testament shows one church with one face, though assembled in various locations. This church experienced the supernatural with Holy-Spirit miracles. This church had a governmental ministry order, which is so different from today. We are to understand and follow this holy written example. The Bible has not changed; people have.

We no longer esteem Christ's giving of the five ministry callings, the apostle, prophet, teacher, evangelist and pastor. Jesus our Lord said we need all five of these callings he gives. We need to discern these and receive all five working in unity to mature the church. These callings exist today, but few can properly discern them by their differing burdens and vision. Those who can identify them, have not sought or submitted to flowing in unity under an apostle-led, Christ-given, and orchestrated government. This must be restored.

The genuine apostles must be discerned, and they must arise. They must be received to again lead by establishing Christ's church government, the reestablishing of what has been destroyed by bad doctrine. This is the main cause of the separation that now exists, destroying church unity. This will only be restored by those who fervently seek to apply what the New Testament scriptures portray. We speak highly of past reformers who brought correction to dead church religiosity from the 1400s onward. May we now uphold and encourage the reformers of today, who wage war while striving to continue the much-needed church reformation.

AN UNCHANGED CHURCH

Sorrow and treason by ignorance being blind,
The treasure of treasures is now so hard to find.
The church that I read of with Holy Ghost power
Is so far from what should be in this final hour.

I searched out the reason to this declined estate—
What brought to change, to our now-current fate?
Bad unscriptural doctrine is the root of our loss,
Man's reasoning, wrong doctrine, these damage the cross.

Written Holy Bible truths must ever be severed—
Jesus Christ is the same yesterday, now, and forever.
Our sovereign Lord reigning, enthroned up above,
Unchanged God of miracles, holy power and love.

Are we content with a church having suffered wrong change?
Or zeal-cloaked reformers now focused to regain?
What we read in the Book of Acts, the blueprint of ministry—
Are we determined to change and restore our church history?

By establishing Christ's giving, His government for today,
Christ's given five callings, to bring order to disarray.
Apostle first headship, prophets and teachers given to lead,
Discerned evangelists and pastors: these must all be received.

Christ is Lord when we obey, as we yield to His Word,
By obedience in church building, these must all be restored.
To again experience holy fire, holy winds with great power,
A renewed church, Christ glorified, true worship in this hour.

(Heb. 13:8, Acts 2:1, 36, 19:11, 1 Cor. 12:10, JDV)

CHAPTER ONE:
Church Ministry and Building

The Church

The church is God's chosen jewel for eternity. Heaven and earth will pass away, but God's redeemed and overcoming saints will spend eternity as Christ's bride in His new heavenly Kingdom. The genuine saved Christian loves God, His church, and unsaved people. The church is what our Lord Jesus seeks, and what He died for. To be Christ's servants, we will be involved with saving souls, maturing believers, and building His church. This church must be built in the manner our Lord and Savior meant when He said, "I will build my church."

We love our God and Savior. From a heart of worship, we now enter into His vision and labors, as we, His servants, build His church. We see God's heart and the needs of our fellow man—spiritual needs, leading to eternal death. To be used of Christ in ministry to build His church is a huge privilege and honor, but it is also a great responsibility.

We must build by using His blueprint, His Holy Word. To build while demonstrating a disregard for what God says by His Word is either due to ignorance or a lack of love for Him. Disregarding His Word in this pinnacle of importance involves a prideful disposition with a self-willed disregard of His Lordship. Those who genuinely make Christ Jesus the Lord of their lives and ministry will deeply search out our Lord's will and His scriptural directions in building.

Today, most ministries miss the mark and fail in this. Real study of God's Word will lead us to numerous truths,.which most ministries disregard. This writing sets out what we in obedience must set in place. When we apply Christ's scripturally given truth and mandates, we will establish what we term a Biblical "fivefold church." This term does not only describe the leadership model; it involves much more, as we consider the ministry of the believer.

Change

Real fivefold ministry realities will only come to those who receive all of God's Word—those who are willing to pay whatever price it takes to experience it. Should this be the case, we will receive the rewards, along with a heavenly Holy Ghost presence, now and forever. This writing is an attempt to present many of the needed truths to achieve this goal.

True revival will only take place when determined ministries and believers are willing to forsake the traditions and heritage of the elders. We must focus strongly on scriptural ministry, the Book of Acts church, and what our believer expectations should be. If the Word says it, we bow with obedience to Christ and do it! Focusing on the key objective in life—our salvation—must be our immense priority. Heaven and earth will pass away, but what we do for and by Christ never will.

Misunderstandings in Building

We waste our time when dealing with this topic of "fivefold church building" unless several absolutes are confronted and applied. Do not waste your time. When we are not prepared to make changes to what normally exists—changes that will affect our personal ministry—we will only be toying with ideology, debate, and rhetoric. To genuinely build what Christ desires, we must believe that the entire Bible is the Word of God. Holy men of old wrote as God when the Holy Ghost moved upon them. God said it, and we believe what is taught and portrayed in the New Testament Book of Acts, as well as all the letters to the churches (2 Pet. 1:21). These holy writings are for what is now meant to be. The prophet Joel said,

> "Be glad then, ye children of Zion, and rejoice in the LORD your God: for he hath given you the former rain moderately, and he will cause to come down for you the rain, the former rain, and the latter rain in the first month. . . . And it shall come to pass

afterward, that I will pour out my spirit upon all flesh; and your sons and your daughters shall prophesy, your old men shall dream dreams, your young men shall see visions: And also upon the servants and upon the handmaids in those days will I pour out my spirit. And I will shew wonders in the heavens and in the earth, blood, and fire, and pillars of smoke. The sun shall be turned into darkness, and the moon into blood, before the great and the terrible day of the LORD come". (Joel 2:23–31)

Why do most churches disregard this prophetic Word? This trend affects what our churches need to experience and believe in. We should agree that no scriptures exist that allow us to bring change by a different approach.

Recently, while ministering, a young lady received a creative miracle. A short limb immediately grew out to match her other limb. Her shocked response was, "My denomination teaches me that these things are no more." I answered, "That is sad, because their denial of Bible scriptures has brought them to disbelief." We must believe God's unchanging Word! We must receive His truth. An experiential baptism of the Holy Spirit with the resulting gifts of the Spirit is for today (Acts 2:39). Also, most churches deny that Christ, upon His ascension, gave five-gift ministries to all of mankind: *"And he gave some, apostles; and some, prophets; and some, evangelists; and some, pastors and teachers; For the perfecting of the saints, for the work of the ministry, for the edifying of the body of Christ"* (Eph. 4:8, 11–12). This giving has not changed.

All must believe the scriptures that deal with Christ's setting in place, of His desired government and authority order in His church: *"But now hath God set the members every one of them in the body, as it hath pleased him. And God hath set some in the church, first apostles, secondarily prophets, thirdly teachers, after that miracles, then gifts of healings, helps, governments, diversities of tongues"* (1 Cor. 12:28). This structure is willfully denied by the majority of ministries and churches.

If we do not esteem our fellow ministries and a plurality of elders in every church, then our focus is unscriptural and filled with error: *"For this cause left I thee in Crete, that you should set in order the things that are wanting, and ordain elders in every city, as I had appointed thee*" (Titus 1:5). A church that does not have a functional multiple eldership ministry is "out of order!"

When we do not pursue the goal of having all elders come to maturity in knowledge and spiritual judgment, how can we release them to oversee the church body? How can we release them to ministry involving spiritual principles by the Word? Paul told the multiple Ephesus "fivefold" elders, "*Take heed therefore unto yourselves, and to all the flock, over the which the Holy Ghost hath made you overseers, to feed the church of God, which he hath purchased with his own blood*" (Acts 20:17, 28). This takes a level of attained maturity.

Until we are prepared to live out the reality of mutual accountability with humility, we will not achieve a fivefold multiple ministry church. We will talk about it, but in reality, we will only have a onefold church. Until we are prepared to submit to each other as believers—and especially as the ministry—we will limit a fivefold church. As the Bible reads, "*Likewise, ye younger, submit yourselves unto the elder. Yea, **all of you** be subject one to another, and be clothed with humility: for God resists the proud, and giveth grace to the humble*" (1 Pet. 5:5). The servant towel and foot-washing demonstration Jesus gave, in no way denies or displaces the placement of Christ's governmental authority order.

When we deny or do not stand strongly for God's ordinances, appointed customs, and doctrines in His church, we will fail in our efforts to build what Christ desires. When we do not desire to see all believers as "ministry," we limit Christ, the people, and our churches. This is lacking in most churches, and it is a great tragedy. The five-gift callings are given to mature the church for ministry; that is what is meant by "*the perfecting* [maturing] *of the saints*" (Eph. 4:12).

When we do not act in humility before God and man, we will pridefully build "our" churches instead of Christ's desired church. When we do not desire to see the Book of Acts today, nor believe for this, reading this book is a waste of consumption for you. We must believe the Holy Bible's written New Testament examples.

As we digest scriptural truths, we need to implement them in our building; there is a terrible, painful loss to the Kingdom of God when they are disregarded. The prophet Ezekiel was told to *"eat the roll of the Book"* before charging out to his God-given ministry (Ezek. 2:8–9). This means he was to digest God's Word, speaking of His heart and plan. This truth applies to our church building; not digesting and applying all New Testament Books as our blueprint will result in a great loss of salvation and Kingdom souls. This currently is the existing reality, due to the lack and immaturity of both leaders and their resulting church body.

"There is one body" (1 Cor. 12:12); yet the great majority of churches speak of two churches. An early church and the current church as being two differing bodies. There is the beginning of the church almost two thousand years ago, but it is the same church and the same one body we all belong to. These deficient preachers say there were only twelve apostles and no more; they disregard the nearly twelve others spoken of in the New Testament, many of whom existed at the same time as the first twelve; for example: *"Paul, and Silvanus, and Timotheus, unto the church of the Thessalonians . . . Nor of men sought we glory, neither of you, nor yet of others, when we might have been burdensome, as the apostles [Paul, Silvanus, and Timotheus] of Christ"* (1 Thess. 1:1, 2:6; Gal. 1:19). There are more.

By ignoring and disregarding this continuance of more apostles, we damage what should be in Christ's church ministry and government. This must be repented of, and then restored.

Some of us lament the painful loss and resulting damage caused by ministry failures; we weep at the damage when Holy Spirit gifted and knowledgeable ministry fall off the cliffs of godly holy standards. This is the result of failure due to one's immorality, pride over their self-image, or financial pursuits. Likewise, similar damage results from fivefold church denial. Before one concludes that this is just a judgmental critique, consider that 90 percent of all who claim to be Christians have never led a soul to Christ. Now assess the reality that 99 percent of "Christians" cannot even name or provide a minor teaching on the Christian foundational doctrines of the Bible. This affects the believers' ministry abilities. This lacking knowledge demonstrates the immaturity of the church in general. We must change this and seek out Biblical church ministry as we build. If we agree to this and confront this truth, we must seek to apply this. All born-of-the-Spirit Christians should choose to be ministry, salt, and light to the world. All should seek to save and mature souls (Dan. 12:3).

In summary, fivefold church building, when compared to all other church building endeavors, is the establishing of what the New Testament portrays—not an unscriptural, different church.

Serious Key Truth

We must seriously digest and deal with our Savior's statement when He said, "*You have a few names even in Sardis which have not defiled their garments; and they shall walk with me in white: for they are worthy*" (Rev. 3:4). We must wholeheartedly bring change to this Bible Word "few," a written fact. Why just a few? Why are not all people in this church allowed to dress in white and walk with Christ? We must thoroughly contemplate why this is as we pursue church building.

When we follow scriptural building with "fivefold church" truth revelations, this painful judgment of "*only a few will walk with me in white*" upon the church, will greatly change. The change will be equal to recovering from the loss resulting from the Roman Catholic Church, not allowing their people to possess and read Bibles until the 1950s. Consider the increase when many adherents experienced receiving a personal salvation after this. The result of genuine evangelical Christian ministry affected this when they preached how by repentance and faith in Jesus and the cross, and not due to our works salvation is attained. Masses were "born again" by the resulting Charismatic Renewal.

Then, also consider the effect of when ministries teach their followings the importance of fruit-bearing, and not to forsake our abiding in Christ. Many believers never hear any messages addressing their responsibility to make their salvation election sure. They only hear that if you are of the elect, then you are guaranteed heaven. Many do not hear teachings of our need to add to our faith (2 Pet. 1:5–9). Many churches do not teach what all should hear. Our Lord Jesus told all of the seven churches and us that in order to receive God's promises given to all of the churches, we must "overcome"; this was spoken to the born-of-the-Spirit churches, and not to the world. God requires our overcoming in the challenges and temptations of life as our hearts are tested (Exod. 16:4; Rev. 2:7, 11, 17, 26, 3:5, 12). If this does not readily meet with your theology, then change your theology. Do not be selective in which scriptures you receive and which you deny.

For those who have difficulty with this presentation, consider what the Apostle Paul said when he quoted the lament of Isaiah. He spoke of God's covenant people. Isaiah said that of those who left Egypt on their forty-year desert journey, only a small remnant reached the Promised Land: *"Esaias also cries concerning Israel, Though the number of the children of Israel be as the sand of the sea, a remnant shall be saved"* (Rom. 9:7). Why were these circumcised covenant people not saved? Why did God in His wrath swear they would not enter into His rest? (Heb. 3:11)

Then we have this dire truth spoken to the church of today: *"Even so then at this present time also there is a remnant according to the election of grace"* (Rom. 11:4–5). This "remnant" refers to the few overcoming believers in the church of Sardis; the rest were denied to walk with Christ for eternity, by having defiled their garments. Why is this the truth and reality?

In Elijah's day, only seven thousand survived spiritually; those who did not change to Baal worship. In church building, what the ministry projects affects our people. A greater *"remnant"* will reach the Promised Land when we are used to increase their knowledge. Today, we limit our churches when we ignore building with the Biblical "fivefold ministry" and the truths they project. We need all five callings. If you doubt this, read the following:

> *"How then shall they call on him in whom they have not believed? and how shall they believe in him of whom they have not heard? and how shall they hear without a preacher? And how shall they preach, except they be sent? as it is written, How beautiful are the feet of them that preach the gospel of peace, and bring glad tidings of good things"*! (Rom. 10:14–15)

We choose to bless preaching and sending. We, Christ's ministry and disciples, are used of God to build the church and reach the multitudes.

All ministry and believers should ponder these scriptures; then they should become part of the answer!

The validity of this will be set out beyond any doubt by this writing, but only for those who will be Bereans (Acts 17:11). Bereans examined all scriptures quoted by Apostle Paul.

Ministry-focused believers who bear fruit will be among those who walk with Christ in heaven. They are dressed in white: *"And to her was granted that she should be arrayed in fine linen, clean and white: for the fine linen is the righteousness of saints"* (Rev. 19:8; Ezek. 44:17). The greater percentage of the Sardis church was denied from wearing this fine linen attire, and from an eternal walk with Christ. The white linen garments exemplified the *"righteousness of saints."* They were denied this (Rev. 19:8); only overcoming saints with non-defiled garments, having overcome a sinful life are granted to wear these. Without this, they are not welcome to heaven's wedding feast (Rev. 3:18; Matt. 22:11).

Those who were granted to wear fine linen were godly focused and mature in their Christ love, prayer walk, and knowledge as they ministered Christ to others. They had no problem with what our Lord also said: *"For whosoever shall be ashamed of me and of my words, of him shall the Son of man be ashamed, when he shall come in his own glory, and in his Father's, and of the holy angels"* (Luke 9:26). Much of the loss is due to not bringing the baby saints to maturity.

Maturity

Please do not disregard or shrink at this statement: a minimum nine out of ten believers are Christian babies, as per the Apostle Paul. Paul judged that most of the Hebrews church were "babes." Paul taught that "baby status" applies to all Christians who are not capable of giving a minor teaching on the six foundational doctrines (Heb. 5:10–6:2). Read this, and then bring change.

A major factor in not maturing believers, is by ignoring what the Bible teaches to mature them. These foundational doctrines are a major part; along with teachings about Christian character (Mt. 5:2-11, 2 Pet. 1:5) Then we ignore Christ our Lord gave five differing ministry callings to teach knowledge and virtue. Most churches refuse to accept or understand this giving. Rather than deny this giving, we must learn how to discern these differing callings; then seek to facilitate them in our churches. All the different callings have priority burdens. All of them have spiritual wealth to impart as they bring the saints to maturity for their ministry. To reiterate: *"And he gave some, apostles; and some, prophets; and some, evangelists; and some, pastors and teachers; 12 For the perfecting* [maturing] *of the saints, for the work of the ministry, for the edifying of the body of Christ"* (Eph. 4:11).

Fivefold churches believe strongly in this "giving" to mature the church; they desire to implement this mostly ignored truth. Hosea spoke God's Holy Words, which truthfully apply to us today: *"My people are destroyed for lack of knowledge: because thou hast rejected knowledge, I will also reject thee, that thou shalt be no priest to me: seeing thou hast forgotten the law of thy God, I will also forget thy children"* (Hosea 4:6). By forgetting and not following God's laws and knowledge, we—and especially our children—suffer the results. How many Christian parents weep over godless children? I ask, did you ground them in foundational doctrine, or did you just take them to church? Did they grow up on the baby-food message of God's love and faithfulness while enjoying a social family? Or did they grow up with the teaching and knowledge that would mature them into being a salt-and-light ministry with ministry priority as a life's focus?

When we do not mature the saints and our children, it greatly affects their lives. When they are denied God's banquet table of the multiple eldership fivefold ministry, they are needlessly impoverished. This denial affects the establishing of the world church. We need a unified ministry flow, which we can achieve by not ignoring the needed five callings. Promote, accept, and encourage the fellow ministry callings our Lord says we need. All of them must be harnessed in unity. Before tractors were invented, people used large horses to clear fields and tree stumps. Should a stump be too hard to be pulled by one horse, multiple horses were harnessed to enable the work. May we learn from this!

Evaluate the results demonstrated by the early church after Pentecost; the explosion of church growth after Pentecost was apostle-led. Today, most churches deny apostles of today and Pentecost to be experienced by all believers. *"For the promise is unto you, and to your children, and to all that are afar off, even as many as the Lord our God shall call"* (Acts 2:39).

Thousands of people were added in the following weeks and months. The unbelieving world complained that these believers *"turned their world upside down"* (Acts 17:6). This early church explosion resulted from the first of nine listed truths following Pentecost: *"And they continued steadfastly in the apostles' doctrine and fellowship"* (Acts 2:42). What was their diet of receiving a*postle's doctrine?"* It behooves us to examine this truth. This exemplifies God's Holy Word to us. Great failure is evident from an honest minimal review of all churches and history. Millions are steeped in religiosity, but they have never experienced being "born of the Spirit," which is a basic must (John 3:5, Rom. 8:9).

Building Understandings

We love Christ, and we must also love the church. To successfully build Biblical fivefold New Testament churches, ministries will need to focus on several maturities, such as the following:

a) Review the scriptures. Christ gives five differing gift ministries to the entire church; no scriptures exist or support that this giving was only for a limited time (Eph. 4:8, 11).

b) Seek out the five callings. This takes an education. Learn how to discern these five callings. Our Savior commended the church of Ephesus when He said, *"I know thy works, and thy labor, and thy patience, and how thou canst not bear them which are evil: and thou hast tried them which say they are apostles, and are not, and hast found them liars"* (Rev. 2:2).

c) We deny His Lordship when we build churches without a multiple, growing, and maturing eldership; the refusal to believe and apply this is proven to be rebellious and wrong. These elders respected the Apostle headship, *"And from Miletus he sent to Ephesus, and called the elders of the church"*; they came (Acts 20:17). This is the Bible truth: a plurality of ministry elders in every church. Most elders are not of the five-gift callings. The Holy Ghost places eldership desire within people and then matures them (1 Tim. 3:1).

d) We must expect and discern the workings of the Holy Ghost in our fellow men and elders. Apostle Paul said, *"Take heed therefore unto yourselves, and to all the flock, over the which the Holy Ghost hath made you overseers, to feed the church of God, which he hath purchased with his own blood"* (Act 20:28). All of the elders are to feed (referring to the sharing of Word and personal ministry) and not just oversee.

e) Apostles and teachers, more than other callings, will excel in doctrinal maturity. Due to not identifying and liberating these callings, less than 1 percent of church attendees are capable of naming the foundational doctrines listed in Hebrews chapter six. Recently, while I was speaking at a leadership conference oversees that was attended by over 180 people, only two attendees could successfully name these. Fivefold ministry churches are about maturing the saints. Their maturity in turn, will be demonstrated by their personal ministry fruitfulness. This will not take place unless a mature multiple eldership brings the saints to maturity. This multiple mature eldership will not coexist or function unless, with humility and love, elders ministry seek out, discern, embrace, and esteem fellow ministry.

f) A character of grace, knowledge, wisdom, patience, and love for the brethren must be genuine among the adherents. Leadership must humbly exemplify this. Others will follow.

g) A father's or a mother's heart for the believers is a mature ministry virtue; this refers to a heart filled with love to nurture, impart knowledge of the Word and spiritual principles with gentle protective care rather than organizational abilities or a parading of "look at me."

h) All churches without a multiple ministering eldership are "out of order" (Titus 1:5).

i) Ministries must achieve the grace to see the huge value of fellow ministries; then they must also know that all believers are to be ministry.

j) Our value of fellow elders will include financial considerations and practical care for one another (to be discussed later on). Esteeming fellow elder is demonstrated by giving ministry opportunities for all fellow eldership and believers. They grow while they exercise their Holy Spirit given ministry burden and vision. Do that, or do not name them elders. An advisory board is not a Biblical eldership.

k) The most difficult maturity is the humility required to esteem one another with what I term "mutual accountability." The only CEO or top manager of the church is Jesus Christ our Lord. He gives five callings and elders through the workings of the Holy Spirit (Acts 20:28; Phil. 2:13). God the Holy Ghost raises up genuine eldership. Do not squash or squander His workings in the body.

Also; we must strive to promote and make opportunity for the church body membership in their ministry. This means encouraging all believers to function in ministry; however, do not expect that this will happen if we do not mature them with the foundational doctrines. We limit their ministry when we are satisfied with our onefold gifting. Mature the believers for their ministry, both inside and outside the church. A rooter has a needed toolbox, but he must know how to use it. In the same way, foundational doctrine is a large part of the toolbox we need to mature us for ministry.

Anointing Presence

When we speak of "anointing," we refer to the flow of the Holy Ghost's ministry impartation. This is achieved not only by the giving of gifts by the laying on of hands, but also by anointed Holy Bible Word revelation.

All must grow and seek Holy Ghost presence. More than just a claim to heaven by the cross; gaining a salvation relationship is only the entrance to what is now possible. We enter through Christ, the door. Then this initiates and enables our growth and a glorious ministry journey after we entered, beyond the door; Holy Spirit presence and a glorious walk with God. Our ministry is achieved by personally seeking godly knowledge. We must desire Christ's person and Word. We limit God's presence when we do not, with obedience and with a humble heart of worship, uphold Godly principles (His "laws and statutes"). All demonstrated anointing comes from eating at God's table, within His inner court.

How important is the upholding of this? In chapter forty-four, Ezekiel was given holy direction to discern why many are denied presence anointing. This is HUGE! We will read and digest this chapter since this greatly applies to fivefold church building. A lack of manifest anointing and the

Holy Spirit's presence is evidenced in most churches. This is proven by the absence of anyone being healed of sickness; the absence of miracles; and the absence of people being deeply touched by prophetic revelation.

These life-giving streams of the supernatural waters should flow from ministry and from believers; out of your belly it shall flow, due to what you have digested (John 7:38). This flow will stem from those who are welcome and have spent time eating from God's holy table.

Unfortunately, the painful truth today is that many are barred from God's inner court. Many are not welcomed at His table. Why is this? The answer lies in ministries and churches not standing in defense of God's "ordinances and laws" nor seeking these. God's ordinances are of KEY importance to build fivefold churches!

CHAPTER TWO:
Few Welcome in God's Inner Court

Two Kinds of Ministry and Churches

There are two kinds of ministers and churches. Some are welcomed in God's inner court to receive from His table. Many are not since only ordinance keepers are welcomed. The greater majority of churches are ministered to by ministry who are under God's judgment due to neglecting God's ordinances. God gives them their placement of authority. They do His ministry work, but always while being under His judgment. They perform the normal church ministry duties. They are a genuine called and appointed ministry, just as the Levites of old, BUT they are not welcome in God's inner court, nor to eat at His table! We should seek to understand why is this God's placement and His judgment.

The painful truth is that most ministry do not even know they minister while being under God's judgment. Just like David, they desire God's presence. David failed to bring the ark, representing God's presence, home to Jerusalem. Only when He followed God's ordinances did he succeed in doing this.

David as ministry today, did not understand why God did not bless his effort and worship with thirty thousand men. Then God in anger killed Uzzah. Uzzah touching the ark [not a priest] was the last straw that broke god's patience. Like David, we are bereft of bringing God's presence home. We are defeated as well until we understand the truth of this past event. People under ministry leadership of those who do not understand God's judgment upon Uzzah, will also be denied and robbed of God's presence anointing. They follow the ministry they have placed over themselves and are robbed of denied Bible ordinances. When the blind lead the blind, they both fall into the ditch (Matt. 15:14).

Do not wilt at this statement; rather, pursue the basis of this painful scriptural fact. My desire is to see all churches and ministries become welcome and blessed with God's anointing and presence. We must remove God's judgment. How do we do this? We seek and then implement God's ordinances.

Bible Truths Regarding Church Ministry and the Fruit of Error

Pursuing fivefold truths will remove error. To gain insight into this topic, we must pursue a very difficult truth. Today, we must understand, analyze, and do what God ordered His prophet, Ezekiel, to do. This holy mandate equally applies to us now. Understanding this mandate will determine whether or not we are gloriously welcome in God's inner court. After studying these scriptures, ask yourself, "AM I WELCOME? Am I and my church allowed in inner court and presence ministry as we build? Am I dry with thirst because of the drought that exists while not knowing why?" The drought is due to not dealing with the issue of God's "ORDINANCES."

Divine Ordinances

Ezekiel's mandate (AS WELL AS OURS) is that we are to diligently mark, observe, and analyze: "*And the LORD said unto me, Son of man, mark well, and behold with thine eyes, and hear with thine ears all that I say unto thee concerning all the **ordinances** of the house of the LORD, and all the **laws** thereof; and mark [MARK]well the entering in of the house, with every going forth of the sanctuary* " (Ezek. 44:5). Blindly following and not doing this has a cost.

Heed God's mandated instruction to Ezekiel and us. Ezekiel was to observe and study God's appointed, who are called the "Levite ministry." As Ezekiel, we today are to study ministry and what the covenant people of Israel are doing—those who enter and gather in His house, both then and now. Study our church and the leadership of today. Are God's "ordinances and laws" being observed?

Some will say that was Old Testament Israel; not so. Consider this: *"For I am the LORD, **I change not**; therefore ye sons of Jacob are not consumed"* (Mal. 3:6). God has not—and does not—change. The New Testament church has changed. We no longer keep the ceremonial laws as they depicted the Lamb of God to come; Christ fulfilled this. We have a new covenant, by the circumcision of the heart due to our being born of the Spirit. They were not (John 7:39).

Today, we are the Israel of God: *"For in Christ Jesus neither circumcision avails anything, nor uncircumcision, but a new creature. And as many as walk according to this rule, peace be on them, and mercy, and upon the Israel of God"* (Gal. 6:15–16). This "Israel" refers to New Testament born-of-the-Spirit believers.

Spiritually speaking, we are the children of Abraham: *"Therefore it is of faith, that it might be by grace; to the end the promise might be sure to all the seed; not to that only which is of the law, but to that also which is of the faith of Abraham; who is the father of us all"* (Rom. 4:16).

Mark Well: God Wants Us to See and Hear

The command to *"mark well, and behold with thine eyes, and hear with thine ears"* is of equal importance now. Are we comparing our beliefs and church gatherings to the churches we read about in the New Testaments? The priority study of *"the **ordinances** of the house of the LORD, and all the **laws** thereof"* is what we are to observe. We are to wear Bible truth glasses as we observe. We must use these as we *"mark well the entering in of the house, with every going forth of the sanctuary."* Are we keeping God's *"**ordinances** of the house of the LORD, and all the **laws** thereof"*? We must have knowledge of "ordinances and laws".

This commandment to Ezekiel reveals how the Lord is constantly observing us, in our dealings in life, and how our ministry affects His loved and treasured church. This truth of our God telling us to observe and mark well demonstrates the omniscient, all-seeing knowledge and eyes of the Lord over all souls—and especially His church:

a) *"For the eyes of the LORD run to and fro throughout the whole earth, to shew himself strong in the behalf of them whose heart is perfect toward him"* (2 Chron. 16:9).
b) *"I know thy works, and thy labor, and thy patience, and how thou canst not bear them which are evil"* (Rev. 2:2).
c) *"Known unto God are all his works from the beginning of the world"* (Acts 15:18).

What are God's ordinances and laws? When we are limited in the knowledge and application of God's ordinances and laws, our truth-magnifying glasses will be obscured with the film of lack of knowledge. We need clear glasses of knowledge as we diligently discern, *"mark well,"* or study what proceeds out of God's house of worship, His church.

Note: This was not a study of the unbelievers or the world, but rather of God's Levitical ministry and His circumcised covenant people. This now applies to circumcised hearts (Phil. 3:3; Col. 2:11).

God's Complaint

When God expresses His judgments and gives the reasons for them, we must pay attention as this written to Ezekiel and us:

> *"And thou shalt say to the rebellious, even to the house of Israel, Thus says the Lord GOD; O ye house of Israel, let it suffice you of all your abominations, In that ye have brought into my sanctuary strangers, uncircumcised in heart, and uncircumcised in flesh, to be in my sanctuary, to pollute it, even my house, when ye offer my bread, the fat and the blood, and they have **broken my covenant** because of all your abominations. And ye have not kept the charge of mine holy things: but ye have set keepers of my charge in my sanctuary for yourselves."* (Ezek. 44:6–8)

To the rebellious Israel of that time, and also to the people of today, God says the people *"set keepers of my charge in my sanctuary for yourselves."* The people attended, kept the ceremonial religious practices while God says, *"they have broken my covenant."* How can this be? They set uncircumcised heart of ministry over themselves—ministry that claim to be God's reverend or bishop, but a ministry who have disregarded God's **"ordinances and laws."**

What are God's ordinances? (Strong's Concordance, Hebrew Dictionary definition for ordinances is "appointed manner, custom, and statutes). By ignoring the appointed statutes, God's judgment is upon this church, ministry, and people.

> *"Thus says the Lord GOD; No stranger, uncircumcised in heart, nor uncircumcised in flesh, shall enter into my sanctuary, of any stranger that is among the children of Israel. And the Levites that are gone away far from me, when Israel went astray, which went astray away from me after their idols; they shall even bear their iniquity"* (Ezek. 44:9–10).

The uncircumcised of heart need to become circumcised of heart (circumcision depicted the message of a daily reminder, to have our works and what we produce in uncloaked transparency when we sow). This scripture also speaks to judgment upon negligent ministry.

God-Given Mandates Are Nonnegotiable

Let's take the gloves off and be real. In some measure, many are guilty of what Samuel said to Saul: *"For rebellion is as the sin of witchcraft, and stubbornness is as iniquity and idolatry"* (1 Sam. 15:23, 3). Saul had not fulfilled what the Lord had told him to do, which was to *"destroy Amalek and all of what pertains to Amalek."* (1 Sam. 15:3).Today, we are equally guilty as we selectively ignore God's scriptures that speak to his ministry and desired government. As Saul, we act in rebellion to God's Word when we deny what we term as "fivefold ministry" truths.

God's dealings with us will always reveal grace and goodness, but also His severity: *"Behold therefore the goodness and severity of God: on them which fell, severity; but toward thee, goodness, if thou continue in his goodness: otherwise thou also shalt be cut off"* (Rom. 11:22). Therefore, God reveals both heaven and mercy, hell and His coming eternal judgment.

Again, from the life and experiences of David, we see a great scriptural example of God's firm stance of disdain for those who disregard His ordinances. King David loved God and His presence. This presence included manifestations of dreams and visions, angelic and prophet visitations, and being under a cloud anointing, just as Israel experienced in the desert. The priests could not stand due to this cloud presence.. We call this being "slain in the Spirit".

David greatly esteemed the ark of God as a holy temple artifact. The ark represented the presence of God. The ark was covered by His mercy seat. The mercy seat spoke to our mercy being available. When Christ ascended He placed His blood there. (He. 9:7-12) While the ark was present in the house of Obededom, the Lord greatly blessed him (2 Chron. 6:11).

David attempted to bring the ark to Jerusalem with great preparations by gathering thirty thousand chosen men of Israel to accompany the ark. He placed it on a new specially built wooden cart. They made a huge effort of presenting worship in music, as described in Samuel:

> "And David and all the house of Israel played before the LORD on all manner of instruments made of fir wood, even on harps, and on psalteries, and on timbrels, and on cornets, and on cymbals. And when they came to Nachon's threshing floor, Uzzah put forth his hand to the ark of God, and took hold of it; for the oxen shook it. And the anger of the LORD was kindled against Uzzah; and God smote him there for his error; and there he died by the ark of God". (2 Sam. 6:5–7).

Uzzah died by God's judgment. God's grace was stretched to the limit. God made a statement of Divine displeasure, when He brought judgment to express this. Uzzah defiled priesthood truth. The ark did not come home to Jerusalem that day, BUT it eventually did.

Why not, then? What changed? David sought out "God's ordinance." He researched how to bring the ark and God's presence home; may we do likewise. David acknowledged his fault. God never judges *"Uzzah"*—or us—without reason. As it reads in 1 Chronicles:

"For because ye did it not at the first, the LORD our God made a breach upon us, for that we sought him not after the due order. So the priests and the Levites sanctified themselves to bring up the ark of the LORD God of Israel. And the children of the Levites bare the ark of God upon their shoulders with the staves thereon, as Moses commanded according to the word of the LORD". (1 Chron. 15:13–15)

Is the Lord making *"a breach upon us"* today? Like David, we must research "our due order" and search out why God's presence, blessings, and His healing miracles and prophecies are limited. God's due order was that only the chosen Levite priesthood are to carry the ark on their shoulders. Today, we no longer have the Levitical priesthood. We have our new *"due order"*: Christ's giving of the five differing ministry callings. These, as per His appointment and Word, are the *"set some in the church"* He gives and is ignored (1 Cor. 12:28).

Are we building our wooden carts, the perfection of choir voices, instruments and church décor being focused on gathering thirty thousand while defiling God's ministry ordinances?

Likewise Today

Today, we need to seek and establish His divine order! Presence, anointing, and massive growth will result from church building following God's given fivefold ministry government. We must stop building wooden carts, and we must bring home God's blessings. Yield to Him and receive His Word.

David and the people of Israel desired the presence of God. This presence was embodied in the Ark of the Covenant. Regardless of their worship and the efforts made by David and thirty thousand men to bring the ark home to Jerusalem, they failed. God displayed His anger due to Israel ignoring His divine "ordinances." Are we obeying God's ordinances?

God's blessing on Obededom will likewise come to us when we honor and uphold His ordinances. God's demonstrated presence will manifest when we seek and follow His "ordinance of fivefold ministry church government." When we deny and do not seek out His gifts to us and mankind,

His appointed priesthood for His church, and His given fivefold ministry, his ordinances and appointed customs are desecrated.

God's Judgment

This judgment upon Uzzah should give us some insight into what is occurring today. *We have powerless ministry today because of denied Bible ordinances. God said,:*

> " *Yet they shall be ministers in my sanctuary, having charge at the gates of the house, and ministering to the house: they shall slay the burnt offering and the sacrifice for the people, and they shall stand before them to minister unto them. Because they ministered unto them before their idols, and caused the house of Israel to fall into iniquity; therefore have I lifted up mine hand against them, says the Lord GOD, and they shall bear their iniquity"*
> (Ezek. 44:11–12)

God's judgment came due to the idols that the ministry had in their hearts. Their idol in ministry was to be acceptable to the people while ignoring God's statutes. They did not hold a standard of righteousness when the people went astray. Number of followers, their stature, and their visibility in the ministry was of greater importance to them than what God called them for. God judged them accordingly. His judgment was that they should be in a position of authority and do all of His ministry functions while having a huge limitation.

This major and important truth is missed by most ministries and their followings. They minister by God's command, but always while being under His judgment, and the people as well due to their choice by unstudied recklessly choosing to follow them.

GOD'S JUDGMENT! "*AND they shall NOT come near unto me, to do the office of a priest unto me, nor to come near to any of my holy things, in the most holy place: but they shall bear their shame, and their abominations which they have committed. But I will make them keepers of the* *charge of the house, for all the service thereof, and for all that shall be done therein"* (Ez. 44:13–14).

They will function in ministry, but they will not be allowed *"to come near to any of my holy things, in the most holy place."* How many churches, ministries, and people are affected by God's judgment today? What divine ordinances and laws have we not sought out or kept?

Are We a Zadok Priesthood with God's Approval?

The real question involves the fact that a limited number of the called Levitical priesthood were welcomed into God's presence to partake of His table. Are we of this priesthood today? The painful truth is that a limited number of ministry reap the reward of God's approval. As He stated to Ezekiel:

> *"But the priests the Levites, the sons of Zadok, that kept the charge of my sanctuary when the children of Israel went astray from me, they shall come near to me to minister unto me, and they shall **stand before me** to offer unto me the fat and the blood, says the Lord GOD: They shall enter into my sanctuary, and they shall **come near to my table**, to minister unto me, and they shall keep my charge. And it shall come to pass, that when they **enter in at the gates of the inner court**, they shall be clothed with linen garments; and no wool shall come upon them, whiles they minister in the gates of the inner court, and within. They shall have linen bonnets upon their heads, and shall have linen breeches upon their loins; they shall not gird themselves with anything that causes sweat".* (Ezek. 44:15–18)

The Zadok family Levites were given the right to wear linen clothing. This speaks to their being judged as righteous by God (Rev. 19:8). At that time in Israel, only the Levitical priesthood ministry, the family of Zadok, was welcome to enter God's inner court. They were blessed to partake of His table and experience a constant welcome in His holy presence. The greater majority was denied. God blesses obedience and not numbers or quantity of people.

Are We Welcome as Sons of Zadok?

The (God-allowed) sons of Zadok were one family out of the 7,500 Levitical priesthood males of that day. Only the sons of Zadok were welcomed into His inner court, to sit at His table (Num. 3:22). The rest of the priesthood did minister, and also by God's appointment, but always with His judgment upon them.

The question is: are we among those who minister with God's appointment, while also being under His judgment? Why were the sons of Zadok welcomed into holy ground presence of God's inner court? **They were welcomed because** they withstood all others—both their fellow Levites and the people. How did they withstand them? They stood and defended God's holy ordinances and laws.

Those who aren't welcome are the ministry who do not defend the keeping of God's *"ordinances and laws."* God's judgment is that they will minister by His determination, but are barred from entering His inner court. They will minister and be placed in authority by Him; they will preach, serve communion, and do all the ministry functions, but always while being under His judgment. We must understand this truth.

This is a God truth and wake-up call. How many churches and ministries of today are under this judgment while thinking they are doing great?

Aaron ministered while being under God's judgment, but he died the moment his priestly garments were removed (Num. 20:28). It is obvious that most churches and ministries have no desire to search out why they do not experience the supernatural miracles and gifts of the Holy Spirit. They are robbed of the prophet Agabus' ministry, the prophetic revelation gifts.

Fivefold Ministry People:
They Seek and Defend God's Ordinances and Laws

What are the torn and lacking *"ordinances"*—God's appointed customs of today? Fivefold ministry strongly pursues knowing and implementing God's ordinances and ordained customs. Regardless of those who oppose them, fivefold reformers will stand to uphold and defend these God given holy ordinances.

These include personally being born of the Spirit, by repentance of sin, with personal faith in response to hearing the gospel (Eph. 1:13). The baptism of the Spirit with tongues and other gifts of the Holy Spirit is a divine ordinance for Christ's church! Furthermore, when Christ ascended, He gave five differing ministry callings to mature the church. These are some of God's divine ordinances! Jesus Christ is Lord of the church. Christ Jesus our Lord set His ordinance and His appointed custom—His appointed governmental ministry authority. His order is setting apostles first, prophets second, then teachers. This is God's denied ordinance. Establish this! (1 Cor. 12:28) Disobedience to this results in a powerless church, and an anemic or nonexistent ministry by the believer assembly.

Gross error today: For some non-textual or scriptural reason, many deceived churches conclude and believe that the Christ-given five-ministry callings were only for the first one hundred years of our church establishing. They ignore the following: *"Wherefore he says, When he ascended up on high, he led captivity captive, and gave gifts unto men. . . . And he gave some, apostles; and some, prophets; and some, evangelists; and some, pastors and teachers"* (Eph. 4:8, 11). This giving of five differing ministry callings is to all men (humanity); the scripture does not state the words "to SOME men," as many say it does.

Then, in an irrational unqualified manner contrary to this position, they accept a portion of this scripture. The giving and receiving of pastors and evangelists. Then they deny apostles, prophets, and teachers—all of this with no textual rationale for doing so.

I believe that I do understand man's reasonings; this is, how they arrived at this erroneous viewpoint. Since the ministry did not experience supernatural Holy Ghost miracles (healing and prophetic revelation gifts), they denied the callings that should demonstrate these gifts. The root to not seeing the miraculous is the denial of an experiential baptism of the Holy Spirit, as well as man's reasonings destroying what the Word says.

God's Word is unalterable. There are three repeated statements our Lord said to all of the seven churches, and to us, as well. For example, seven times our reigning Savior said, *"I know your works."* (Rev. 2:2, 9)

Also, seven promises are received by those *"who overcome,"* which is achieved by the *"blood of the lamb, and the words of our testimony"* (Rev. 12:11; Eph. 1:13). Our testimony and Words must be consistent with Christ and His Words of truth.

Ignoring the serious truths revealed in scriptures is one of the main reasons for why we see a powerless church today—a church that's much different from what we read about in the New Testament. Because of the gravity of this truth, let us again review the following:

> *"And the LORD said unto me, Son of man, mark well, and behold with thine eyes, and hear with thine ears all that I say unto thee concerning all* **the ordinances of the house of the LORD, and all the laws** *thereof; and mark well the entering in of the house, with every going forth of the sanctuary".* (Ezek. 44:5)

Just like God's servant, Ezekiel, we must strongly observe God's *"ordinances,"* appointed manners, customs, and statutes. Are these being implemented in His church today? If not, repent before our merciful God. Then change this. When we refuse, Samuel's words to Saul apply to us: *"Hath the LORD as great delight in burnt offerings and sacrifices, as in obeying the voice of the LORD? Behold, to obey is better than sacrifice"* (1 Sam. 15:22). Maintaining religious church life has limited value in God's sight when we disobey His *"ordinances."*

The church is the *"apple of His eye,"* His bride company. Beware, however, *"for thus says the LORD of hosts; . . . he that touches you touches the apple of his eye"* (Zech. 2:8). May ministries see the tremendous responsibility of being correct in "church" matters. God given doctrine and holy custom are the epitome of truth; pursue these. God said that those who do not seek, keep, and defend God's ordinances are covenant breakers (Ezek. 44:7).

The circumcised of heart will tremble at God's Word, AND the Lord will appear to them:

> *"For all those things hath mine hand made, and all those things have been, says the LORD: but to this man will I look, even to him*

that is poor and of a contrite spirit, and trembles at my word. . .
. Hear the word of the LORD, ye that tremble at his word; your
brethren that hated you, that cast you out for my name's sake,
said, Let the LORD be glorified: but he shall appear to your joy,
and they shall be ashamed". (Isa. 66:22, 5)

Those who are welcomed in the inner court are believers who tremble
at God's Word.

Word Strength

Fivefold church building ministries and people must NEVER fear rejection, nor should they fear being ostracized by brethren who do not seek the truths we know to be correct. Honor Christ by keeping His given ministry ordinances. May those who do not understand us have the love and heart to hear and discuss our understanding of the often-disregarded scriptures that we see as relevant.

While writing this morning, I prayerfully woke up, and the Holy Spirit quickened an old song in my mind—one that I had not heard for several decades:

The Son of God went forth to war,
A mighty crown to gain;
His blood-stained banner flows afar,
Who follows in His train?
Who else will drink His cup of woe,
Who else will bear His shame?
The Son of God goes forth to war,
Who follows in His train?

Lord, help us as we build your church! May we repent from our failure; *"ye have not kept the charge of mine holy things: but ye have set keepers of my charge in my sanctuary for yourselves"* (Ezek. 44:8). God holds the people affected by wrongful ministry equally guilty, due to the fact that they set carnal ministry over themselves. Believers must discern godly ministry and holy ordinances; these can be discerned by God's Word.

Are we, His ministry, keeping God's "holy ordinances" in place? Are we content with the church when they are not?

Fivefold Ministry

Christ's ordinance for His church today is the giving of five differing called and appointed ministries. We must be willing to stand against the common rejection and denial of this. We must desire to be obedient to God's Word and His giving, rather than to simply please people. We must despise the pain of any cross and shame, whether silent critique or vocal, when we transgress the customs of the elders. (Mk. 7:8) We must refuse to let the critique and rejection of the ministry, who do not understand this truth, to rent space in our minds (Heb. 12:2). The customs of the elders are, when churches deny upholding God's *"ordinances"* and laws! (Matt. 15:2) The Levites, who erred, yielded to being acceptable to the "status quo" people; they did not want to "rock the boat." They were willing to offend God in order to please the people, because they feared the people's rejection.

FIVEFOLD ministry IS His given ordinance. This is His Word and will—no matter how big the church grows, how capable the worship music is, or how many good programs we may have. When God's ordinance and government of the New Testament church, His giving and placement of fivefold ministry is denied. Do not build "my ministry." Build what Jesus desires when He said, *"I will build my church."* (Matt. 16:18) His church has five different ministry callings. The scriptural church always accepted the headship of apostles, followed by the prophet ministry calling. The church is still being built *"upon the foundation of the apostles and prophets, Jesus Christ himself being the chief corner stone"* (Eph. 2:20).

His apostles, prophets, and teachers are now being denied. Even when they are received, their authority placement is still out of order. Fighting to establish a genuine fivefold ministry church will require a firm stand on God's Word. The establishment of the genuine fivefold ministry will involve bucking the traditional winds. Most of the church and ministry of today have gone astray, just like Israel in Old Testament times. I say this with a strong love for the church, BUT as a called servant of the Lord, I have more love for God than people

I see the existing drought due to lacking holy rain. My heart aches, because I see the meager banquet table robbed of genuine spiritual treasure. The starving church is in disarray. Through eyes of faith filled with God's Word, I see what can and should be. DO YOU?

There is a latter-day church and rain; believe and seek this. *"Ask ye of the Lord rain in the time of the latter rain; so the Lord shall make bright clouds, and give them showers of rain, to every one grass in the field"* (Zech. 10:1). Pentecost was only the early rain. Now we must seek the latter rain.

The apostle James, the Lord's brother, admonished us (the church) with the following: *"Be patient therefore, brethren, unto the coming of the Lord. Behold, the husbandman waits for the precious fruit of the earth, and hath long patience for it, until he receive the early and latter rain"* (James 5:7). The early rain is past. The latter rain of the Holy Spirit is coming, and it will produce a harvest of souls as people weep and cry out with repentance under Holy Ghost conviction. This rain brings glorious faith and renewal with joy! Whenever the rain of the Holy Spirit comes, He always brings winds of revelation and spiritual insight (Eph. 1:17).

The Zadok priesthood withstood the errant Levites who failed to stand and uphold God's ministry ordinances. They were rejected by men, but they were welcomed by our God!

Wrongfully focused ministries will not surrender to our Lord, His Word, and His gifts. They deny His given fivefold authority government. This is proven by their demonstrated prideful disregard as they ignore those who present these above cited scriptures. Praise God. There are a number of Zadok-like ministries and people arising today—those who desire truth and all that God has for them. It is awesome!

Truth Denial

Major Word truths are denied by most churches; be honest and discern this reality. This denial involves those who do not teach that one must be born of the Spirit by a personal choice. Half the church teaches that the Holy Spirit is received upon being baptized as an infant. Their ministry leads their followers into a box canyon entrapment of a non-scriptural unreality (Eph. 1:13); I was born under this theology.

Truth denial involves all evangelicals who deny an experiential baptism of the Holy Spirit separate from the new birth (Acts 2:39). These churches do not experience the wonderful strengthening of Holy-Spirit gifts, such as the prophets confirming the people (Acts 15:32).

Evangelicals and old denominations deny and ignore the two separate scriptural events of receiving the birth and the baptism of the Holy Spirit. The cross was past. The risen Christ breathed on his apostles on the resurrection day, saying, *"receive the Holy Ghost"* as they were born of the Spirit (John 20:22). Then he told these same disciples to wait for *"the promise of the Father"* to be endued with power fifty days later (Luke 24:49). This was received at Pentecost, attended by supernatural tongues and prophecy. Peter then told us, *"For the promise is unto you, and to your children, and to all that are afar off, even as many as the Lord our God shall call"* (Acts 2:39). This conscious denial of Christ's breathing on disciples and saying, *"receive the Holy Ghost"* prior to Pentecost, is a theological travesty. This also includes an unscriptural limiting of the Joel promise, to only a first-generation New Testament church—a horrible tragedy (Joel 2:28).

Then, these churches (including the stubborn Pentecostal denominational preacher) disregard the Bible-stated, Christ-given multiple ministry gifts. Let us not leave out the ministries who say they believe in fivefold teachings but continue to practice their onefold focus. The seeking of holy fivefold truths is pursued by a limited company of believing disciples. I prophesy that the church will be restored; the holy wind is blowing, bringing new life and revelation to those who are seeking!

The cost to gospel pursuits: Yes, our Lord is gracious, patient, and long suffering with tender mercy. Yes, He is graciously working in the lives and ministry of all of His churches. However, the limiting of inner sanctuary presence is readily seen everywhere, by powerless ministry. Those who hunger for more will seek the Holy Spirit's presence and anointing. What is our careless lack of seeking His Word-given ordinances costing us? What is this costing the Kingdom? How can we we pray for His Kingdom to be on earth and deny His government?

CHAPTER THREE:
Correction Needed

THE MUCH NEEDED TRUTH:

WHAT makes the church ministry and believers think that God acts differently in today's church? He will bless us as he did Israel, even though they had much error; however, their errors limited His blessing. Until we search out and follow His ministry's order and ways, we will be limiting the blessings of His presence. Things are no different from when David tried to bring the presence blessing—represented by the ark—home. Just as then, we now build ornate churches and have the best types of instruments and hallelujah worship, but this is all done with a limited amount of anointing and presence manifestation—at least, much less than what we read about in our New Testament examples (1 Cor. 14:26).

Much of this is due to not honoring God's gift of ministry government. Instead, we just keep on building wooden carts. Then we try to improve the wooden carts with the worship and décor theatrics. Millions of Christians have never seen a miracle or a holy anointing visitation. Genuine apostles and prophets will minister in gifts of the Spirit as they mature. However, just as Christ was, they will be limited by the recipients of their ministry (Mark 6:5); unbelief and jealousy will hinder the anointing manifestations.

I asked the Lord why I see more Holy-Spirit ministry in some places than others. My answer: some people in leadership have a wrong-heartedness towards others being used in gift anointing. They fear their personal image by comparing themselves to others ministering in these. Thereby they remain limited in personal Holy-Spirit ministry.

I know anointing and holy gift manifestations take more than just having the correct ministry order. It also takes a right-hearted holy ministry with a holy worship focus. It takes a holy people who desire holy presence. When we tolerate Achan and sin in the camp, we will lose our battles (Josh. 7:1–12).

When we decide to set God's holy-given ministry in order, and we pray with humility for a Holy-Spirit presence, He will manifest! Release God's ministry. Why would God deal differently with us than He did David? Release God's order! God has not changed. We, the present churches, have changed. Presence anointing comes though seeking holy inner court presence. This will be possible when our obedience is greater than our sacrifices: *"Behold, to obey is better than sacrifice, and to hearken than the fat of rams"* (1 Sam. 15:22).

Several truths are necessary in order for fivefold ministry blessings to become a reality. If we leave out one of these, we will limit our achievement of what the New Testament Bible churches portray:

a) We must have an absolute faith in the Bible, treating it as the infallible Holy Word of God and as entirely relevant today. This includes all scriptures: both the Old and New Testaments. We must study and learn why there are differing translations of the Bible. Is God's Holy Word, which trumpets salvation, not worth time and effort? We must strongly accept Christ as the Lord of our lives and ministry. He is the Lord of the church. We humbly follow His dictates (Eph. 5:23). Therefore, we must humbly kneel in worship at his Lordship and His Word. Obedience to His Word means we search out His will.

b) We must believe in an experiential "baptism of the Holy Spirit"; usually, this experience is separate from being "born of the Spirit," and fivefold ministry will not function without it. "Baptism of the Holy Spirit" is usually received by having "hands laid on them" by others who have experienced it (Acts 19:6).

c) We must believe that the "gifts to men" that Christ gave us after His ascension are continually being given, as per His promise. Know and believe. There are no scriptures that exist that speak of any time limit to this giving. Christ gave to men (mankind) *"apostles, prophets, evangelists, pastors and teachers"* (Eph. 4:8, 11). Wrongful denial of this truth must be aggressively challenged and withstood. To embrace Bible's truth regarding this important topic, we must personally study and conclude that any who deny this truth are wrong.

d) Christ, as Lord, sets these ministry callings in a governmental author-ity order (1 Cor. 12:18, 28).

e) All churches are to be apostle-led, with a received apostle oversight.

f) The responsibility of the eldership is to mature the saints with knowl-edge and doctrine.

g) We must believe that churches without a multiple functional elder-ship are lacking. As Paul taught, *"set in order the things that are lacking and ordain elders in every city"* (Titus 1:5). This will include elders who are not of the five callings (1 Tim. 3:1). This involves the study of ordination. Understand "what," "who," and "when" in holy ministry dealings.

h) We must be knowledgeable as to how a multiple eldership flows together.

i) We need to learn how to discern the ministry callings.

j) We must gain knowledge of and exercise servanthood in church finances. This affects our ministry relationships: *"Look not every man on his own things, but every man also on the things of others. 5 Let this mind be in you, which was also in Christ Jesus"* (Phil. 2:4).

k) We must confront and learn how to deal with sin. We must know that "a little leaven leavens" the entire loaf (1 Cor. 5:6; Gal. 2:11, 6:1).

l) We must agree that the salvation of our souls is the greatest critical issue in the heart and mind of God. Therefore, this must also be *our* greatest priority in ministry. Then we must agree that we need to dis-ciple and mature the saints. This will lead to the fruitfulness of their ministries; this is of equal importance.

m) Correct doctrinal beliefs are mandatory in the maturing of the saints. Unity will result. It will take time, communication, and open study sessions to achieve this.

n) Building a genuine fivefold church in obedience to Christ and His Lordship will require that we withstand what exists. We must change what is now traditionally accepted.

o) We must place a strong importance on a correct fivefold church ministry government; this is a Christ-given authority order, and it must also be Christ-directed. This government is not possible if we do not learn how to discern the differing ministry callings. We must understand and teach the given authority order (1 Cor. 12:18, 28). To achieve this, we must first kneel to the holy authority of Christ Jesus—both to Him and His WORD!

p) We must practice mature accountability to others. Then, with respect, we must take responsibility for those we oversee. We must have a mutually submissive attitude to all, yet we must know our given authority. Never give in to exercising (or tolerating) a spirit of control. God hates this (Rev. 2:6). Exhort, appeal, plead, and guide as God does, but allow people their choices, even when they are bad choices. We keep order. We set people free to follow and obey, yet we also stand firm to upholding godly conduct. We know the Holy Spirit convicts and draws us to God (John 16:8). We may have to exhort and rebuke in some cases. We may also need to separate the rebellious and unteachable.

q) As much as we desire to keep peace with all men, this must never be at the expense of forfeiting truth: *"Think not that I am come to send peace on earth: I came not to send peace, but a sword. For I am come to set a man at variance against his father, and the daughter against her mother"* (Matt. 10:34–35, Heb. 12:14). Those who follow Christ by seeking His will and glory will be a sword-wielding Holy Word believer.

r) We must have a scriptural understanding of the believer's ministry and their responsibility. Most people today have a very limited understanding of (or expectation of) the believer's ministry (will be enlarged upon).

s) A renewal of how we conduct our services, which should be according to 1 Corinthians, chapter fourteen.

t) Most callings see their own ministry as the priority. Do not wear blinders to fellow elders. Our ministry example will affect and can limit how believers view their ministry.

u) Determined reformers will pursue change. Godly change involves forsaking any tradition or custom that goes against (or is deficient from) what is scripturally portrayed. Bringing change demands a death of our self-image and the fear of man! Only by prostrating ourselves before Christ and His Lordship will we achieve such change.

v) Our conclusion must be that what the New Testament portrays is for today! A church with power and holy unity: this must be our reality now. Acknowledging this need births an Isaiah-type determination within me: *"For Zion's sake I will not be silent, and for Jerusalem's sake I will not rest, until its righteousness goes out as brightness, and her salvation as a burning lamp. And the nations will see your righteousness, and all kings your glory"* (Isa. 62:1–2).

w) Reformation will only be accomplished by those who determine to destroy and overthrow any doctrine or ministry model that limits Christ's truth and Lordship: *"Then the LORD put forth his hand, and touched my mouth. And the LORD said unto me, Behold, I have put my words in thy mouth. See, I have this day set thee over the nations and over the kingdoms, to root out, and to pull down, and to destroy, and to throw down, to build, and to plant"* (Jer. 1:9–10). Note: this mandate will only be carried out by those whose mouths have been touched by our Lord; these people know their Godly Christ-given commission. They are "reformers." They are willing to pay the costs resulting from our tearing down. They destroy whatever is wrongfully built, and then they will plant on this holy cleansed soil.

THAT WHICH IS OUTLINED ABOVE; is the focus of this writing. This is my God-given apostle's ministry mandate and burden, which has been prophetically confirmed by strangers and Holy-Spirit visitations. Many other are rising who share and pursue this mandate!

Required Knowledge, Focus, and Discernment

Most churches deny an experiential "baptism of the Holy Spirit"; they reject the scriptures regarding the five appointed Christ-given callings and government. Those who receive these scriptural callings have many questions about receiving and implementing these truths. How do we discern the genuine callings? How do the callings work in our church of today? Churches are rising that agree to the scriptural fivefold truth; they know change is needed. To achieve needed change will challenge us to let go of things we are currently clinging on to.

There are several interrelated truths that are needed in order to have an experiential fivefold church. All applicable truths need to be identified, studied, and understood. Lacking even one of the applicable truths will diminish our chance at achieving what our Lord desires. The body of Christ has lost the blessings portrayed in the early churches and the Book of Acts. OH LORD! May we be cloaked with your zeal as our garments. May the truths of your Word consume us! We, your servants, desire to establish an obedient holy and righteous church!

Our Savior always knew the purpose and cost of His mission for us. When we know our mission and cost, we, as Christ, will also dress ourselves for battle: *"He put on righteousness like a breastplate, and a helmet of salvation on His head. And He put on the garments of vengeance for clothing, and was covered with zeal like a cloak"* (Isa. 59:17). Knowing and establishing Holy Truth in the face of a Pharisaical religious world requires our prayerful determination.

Rebuilding Must Be Our Vision

Building a functional fivefold church requires a holy vision. Jerusalem was vacated. The temple was looted and left as a burned skeleton. Israel was scattered in judgment for their continual sin. Nehemiah prayed and sought the Lord. By God's favor, he gained the King's favor and a decree to rebuild the temple (read Nehemiah, chapters 1-3). Nehemiah took leaders by night to see the ruins:

> *"And I arose in the night, I and some few men with me. . . . And I went out by night by the Valley Gate, even before the Jackal Fountain, and to the Dung Gate, and looked at the walls of Jerusalem which were broken down, and its gates which were burned with fire. . . . And I said to them, you see the distress that we are in, how Jerusalem is wasted, and the gates of it are burned with fire. Come and let us build up the wall of Jerusalem, so that*

we may no more be a reproach. . . . 18 And I told them of the hand of my God which was good upon me, and also the king's words that he had spoken to me. And they said, Let us rise up to build. So they made their hands strong for good". (Neh. 2:12–18)

Arise. We must review our temple ruins in our existing night. Do we see our burnt gates? These gates speak of the entering in and going out of the people and the effect of our ministry.

May we see, rebuild, and sow the vision of a scriptural ministry government! We must see our broken temple with the destroyed gates. We must decide to rebuild what is needed with the good hand of God upon us—rebuild what was torn, burned, and broken down. We must decry the onefold ministry when we see the way this has neglected our scriptures.

Our Building

We must have faith in God's Word when it tells us that Christ gave gifts to mankind: specifically, the five differing callings. We must acknowledge the Christ-given mandate to mature the church. As it reads in Ephesians:

"And truly He [HE] gave some to be apostles, and some to be prophets, and some to be evangelists, and some to be pastors and teachers, for the perfecting of the saints, for the work of the ministry, for the edifying of the body of Christ. And this until we all come into the unity of the faith and of the knowledge of the Son of God, to a full-grown man, to the measure of the stature of the fullness of Christ; so that we no longer may be infants, tossed to and fro and carried about by every wind of doctrine, in the dishonesty of men, in cunning craftiness, to the wiles of deceit".
(Eph. 4:11–14)

Wrong scholars ignore *"until we all come into the unity.* Where is this "unity" today?

The matured churches do ministry works. Every joint is to supply edification to the body of Christ. To not see this as a scriptural truth for today is a blind, unspiritual, rebellious error! Maturing the church will require this multiple ministry. We must focus, prepare, and expect our church's fellowship gatherings to become conducive to the inclusion of ministry by the church body. This will involve allowing for some people to have a revelation and to operate in using their spiritual gifts (1 Cor. 14:26). Furthermore, it involves demonstrating our faith by conforming to God's Word.

CHAPTER FOUR:
Christ, His Ministry, His Government

WHEN His Government Is Pursued, THEN Christ Is Honored as Head of His Church

Christ is our Lord and God, the Lord of the church. At Pentecost, the Apostle Peter said, "*The LORD said unto my Lord, Sit thou on my right hand, Until I make thy foes thy footstool. Therefore let all the house of Israel know assuredly, that God hath made that same Jesus, whom ye have crucified, both Lord and Christ*" (Acts 2:34–36). Apostle Paul likewise said, "*For the husband is the head of the wife, even as Christ is the head of the church*" (Eph. 5:23).

Christ's Lordship and headship is ignored and rejected when His ministry-giving and government is denied. This is a horrible and spiritual crime! Obedience to His Word by fivefold church building refutes the erroneous, commonly held beliefs that are practiced by most denominations and churches.

A genuine fivefold church strongly believes and pursues the scriptural truths of what our Lord Jesus Christ did upon His ascension: "*Wherefore he says, when he ascended up on high, he led captivity captive, and gave gifts unto men . . . And he gave some, apostles; and some, prophets; and some, evangelists; and some, pastors and teachers*" (Eph. 4:8, 11). God's Word.

It is difficult not to feel frustrated when most deny this scriptural truth. To those I say, as Jesus said to the Sadducees, "*Jesus answering said unto them, Do ye not therefore err, because ye know not the scriptures, neither the power of God?*" (Mark 12:24)

Scriptures do not exist that deny or alter Christ's giving five ministry callings! However, people who changed this do exist. Christ gave gifts to men—not to "some men," as many interpret. The five callings are given to mature and govern His church. Due to the wrongful denial of this gift, an immeasurable loss to the church's establishment and the maturation of the believers has occurred worldwide. Most churches succumb to the lie—which is supported by zero textual evidence—that this act of giving by Christ is only for first-century churches. To reiterate, our Lord Jesus proclaimed his gift to "men" (or "mankind"), and not to "some men." No scriptures exist that support this error. No scriptures exist that demonstrate why we accept pastors and evangelists, while prophets, teachers, and apostles have been ignored.

The correct, Biblical church ministry that Jesus Christ set in order—and His desired government—is hugely important; it is more important than Microsoft, Google, or any other current large corporation. The error is clear; the truth that Christ Jesus had numerous other apostles beyond the original twelve is easily proven. Foolish Bible schools teach that the initial eleven apostles were wrong when they chose Mathias to replace Judas in Acts, chapter one. They teach that the Apostle Paul should have been the twelfth apostle; then there were no more called to this office. These erroneous people are scripturally ignorant because they deny God's Word, which, in truth, speaks of many more apostles. Why do these churches embrace a discontinued apostle and prophet ministry? Here is the evidence:

- *"The apostles, Barnabas and Paul"* (Acts 14:14).
- *"Paul, and Silvanus, and Timotheus, unto the church of the Thessalonians . . . we might have been burdensome, as the apostles of Christ"* (1 Thess. 1:1, 2:6).
- *"But other of the apostles saw I none, save James the Lord's brother"* (Gal. 1:19).
- *"And as we tarried there many days, there came down from Judaea a certain prophet, named Agabus. And when he was come unto us, he took Paul's girdle, and bound his own hands and feet, and said, Thus says the Holy Ghost"* (Acts 21:10–11).

- *"And Judas and Silas, being prophets also themselves, exhorted the brethren with many words, and confirmed them"* (Acts 15:32).

We also ignore, deny, and dishonor Christ's act of giving by not seeking to discern the differences between the five given ministry callings. Our Lord's continual giving applies to all of these callings.

Christ's Giving to Humanity

Our Lord gave five callings by His wisdom and choosing. He is Lord! His Word says he gave all of these with specific intent. As it reads in Ephesians:

> *"And he gave some, apostles; and some, prophets; and some, evangelists; and some, pastors and teachers; For the perfecting of the saints, for the work of the ministry, for the edifying of the body of Christ: Till we all come in the unity of the faith, and of the knowledge of the Son of God, unto a perfect man, unto the measure of the stature of the fullness of Christ".* (Eph. 4:11–13)

Today, by common observation, 99 percent of churches deny this scriptural giving. The reality is that most only rely on a onefold ministry. They do not seek out the apostle and prophet foundation ministry's gifting's or headship.

Our Lord said that we need all of the callings to function and bring the church into maturity. We must not deny this truth as we build Christ's church. We must seek to understand and implement our Lord's wisdom. We must discern how to identify these callings. Seek humble understandings of how they can flow together; this is the reality of the scriptural fulfillment of fivefold church building. This fulfillment will only occur when we, with holy desire, repent and seek to see Christ's church arise. Not just our personal ministry; not my Kingdom, but, "May thy Kingdom come." The saints are robbed of what Christ gives the church when we are unwilling to believe, seek out, and have all five callings available.

Christ's Church Government

Our God is a God of order. He has perfection of order in heaven. There are differences in angelic beings, which is made clear when we read of archangels, seraphs, and lesser angels. In the church—whether in Israel of old or now—God likewise outlines the structure of ministry eldership, government, and order. The Old Testament Levitical priesthood also allowed for the elders that our Lord set in place; then our Lord replaced the priesthood with the New Testament church governmental ministry order: *"But now hath God set the members every one of them in the body, as it hath pleased him. And God hath set some in the church, first apostles, secondarily prophets, thirdly teachers, after that miracles, then gifts of healings, helps, governments, diversities of tongues"* (1 Cor. 12:18, 28).

Where, in the denominational or independent churches, do we find this order functioning? We are the body! A rare few are struggling to observe and achieve this. Most churches deny or rationalize this scriptural truth away. I weep upon seeing this! Where is the humility to God's Word? Where is the releasing of His anointing and power through church eldership? A few onefold gift ministries demonstrate this, while most ignore and deny corporate collegial ministry, as well.

Recently, while visiting a local store, a good Christian brother (who does not attend my anchor church) invited me to come with him to a town some two hundred miles away. His heart's mission is to evangelize the people of this town by giving cold water bottles to migrant workers, thereby facilitating a bridge to share Christ. He is of a soul-gathering mind. My heart rejoices in this. However, my mind instantly went to the reality that you cannot bring babes to the birth and not have them shepherded. One must either bring them to a local church, or establish a church that will feed and shelter them.

We need the multiple ministry structure so it can flow together. We cannot leave birthed babes on the side of the road. Yes, our Lord will take care of all who seek Him, but what is our responsibility to the lambs and sheep? Jesus said to feed and care for them! (John 21:15)

May all of us repent and vow our obedience in accepting and implementing the scriptures; as our Lord Jesus said, *"I will build my church."* How are we used to fulfill this?

Church building is much more than simply pursuing the exactness of an authority order or a power dictatorship. All called ministry should have (and must have) a servant-of-Christ heartedness. Apostle Paul prioritized the humility of his servanthood before he spoke of his ministry calling (Rom. 1:1; Titus 1:1). Being able to discern and witness the multiple callings flowing and manifesting together in unity begins with our reception of the applicable scriptures, as our Lord's Holy Word directs us. Seek to humbly understand and prayerfully facilitate the Holy Word's gifting and strengths. For example, helicopters have unique abilities in warfare usage. However, large jets also have unique abilities. Both are useful in differing ways. It's the same with fivefold ministries. All five callings have unique given differences, as well as strengths imparted by the Holy Spirit. All need to be acknowledged for their differing burdens and visions.

We must return to God's Holy Word—His gifts and orders—by humbly desiring to fulfill His plan. Fulfilling Christ's planned ministry is true worship. Disobedience and rebellion to His Lordship and Word is the root of denial when it comes to establishing a fivefold church. True servants humbly yield to His will while also crushing personal ministry ego and pride.

Government

Our love for Christ is shown when we, with humility, build His church; we are His coming bride who are the precious jewels of the earth (Isa. 43:4). We must seek out how we, as ministry, are to function in the redeeming of man. How do we participate in this building? More importantly, how are others, who are of equal importance, part of this? We must contribute to the team effort in building His church. Building anything less than His fivefold church is an act of ungodly ignorance.

Apostle Paul wrote, "*For we are laborers together with God: ye are God's husbandry, ye are God's building. According to the grace of God which is given unto me, as a wise master builder, I have laid the foundation, and another builds thereon. But let every man take heed how he builds thereupon. For other foundation can no man lay than that is laid, which is Jesus Christ*" (1 Cor. 3:9–11). The corner stone of the foundation upon which all things are measured is Christ Jesus. He gives apostles and prophets as His foundation-building ministry. Apostles lay foundation stones of doctrine and government, while also encouraging all the ministry members. Prophets bring the mortar of holiness that holds these stones together, as well as the gift of God's prophetic revelation. All of the church body is meant to be part of the now-mostly-disregarded *"we"*, that Paul speaks of. All of us are to labor in unison together. Leadership must see to this!

Most churches have a named pastor as the head ministry, whether they are or are not of this calling; this is ignoring what our Lord said. Christ's scriptural governmental order is clearly set out, but it is overlooked by most churches and ministries: *"Now ye are the body of Christ, and members in particular, And God hath set some in the church, first apostles, secondarily prophets, thirdly teachers"* (1 Cor. 12:27–28). We must obey this Holy Word or be in rebellion!

We honor pastors and their calling, but this is not the governmental authority order that our Lord set out. We must seek out how the Christ-given order is to function. Fivefold churches desire to see the Book of Acts depicted now and today. I wince inside when some people speak of their "apostolic" churches. Usually, it is obvious that there is no genuinely called apostle headship. Apostolic churches must seek to flow with a functional apostle headship, properly discerned as such to lead in their ministry.

Apostles themselves will bring faith to new territory. They establish and encourage multiple churches. Humble apostles will desire to see all of the eldership ministries function; not just their own. By denying this Bible-given government, we deny God's authority in His church. We produce an ungodly disorder of multiple guerilla bands instead of a functional army. This disorder is increased by doctrinal limitations. Ignoring these scriptures brings incalculable damage to the church.

The pursuit of restoring fivefold ministry principles is not just some egotistical, unscriptural pursuit. Scriptures do not exist that demonstrate God changed His mind about His giving or His ministry government. Those who deny this are egotistically wrong.

We must identify with Christ in our ministry, vision, and focus. Our purpose is to establish His will. Recently, a "Timothy prophet, a part of my ministry" sent me this sharing:

> And the Government shall be upon His shoulder; ALL Authority given comes from HIM. Kings & Queens, Presidents, Prime Ministers: ALL bow to Him. His Name shall be called: Wonderful, Counselor, The Mighty God, The Everlasting Father, The Prince of Peace. I and the Father are ONE. Behold, before Abraham was, I AM; He was before everything, He is in everything, sees through everything, owns everything, is EVERYWHERE—ALL AT ONCE! Mandates that all things exist simply by putting forth, the utterance of his Word. The Lord Spoke, and the Mountains melted. How can any man, with any level of intelligence and heart, not bow and have tears in his eyes, at the knowledge and revelation of WHO HE IS?

This prophetic utterance hits a deep chord within me. It immediately brings up the prayer of "*may thy Kingdom come upon earth, as in heaven.*" (Matt. 16:18) This evokes a heart prayer of, "I worship you, Almighty God, there is none like you." It creates a deep need in me to bring His church government and ministry into His functional order; currently, it is not!

The church is being built worldwide, and we praise God for His mercy in this. However, the church will be built much faster when it is apostle-led, along with the help of the prophets, who are being released to lay the foundation stones of holiness. The prophet's minister with healing and miracle gifts of the Spirit, and the revelation gifts, where they are received (Matt. 13:57). In his work of church-building, Paul said, "*And are built upon the foundation of the apostles and prophets, Jesus Christ himself being the chief corner stone*" (Eph. 2:20). Today, the church is still being built! We still need all of these callings until Christ returns.

Rebellion: Ignoring God's Government

God dealt with Israel of old. His taking them out of Egypt's bondage is a holy picture given to us. By salvation we are delivered from our past Egypt; the slavery of sin. Seeing the details of the escape from Egypt is more than a lesson in history. Before their deliverance, God prepared chosen vessels to lead His people out of bondage. Moses and Aaron were prepared by the Lord to lead and establish His government among His people. Moses held firm, but Aaron did not, as Aaron followed the people's voice and made golden calves: a perfect example of the dealings in Ezekiel, chapter 44. The moment his priestly garment was taken off, Aaron died. His deferred death arrived. He had been ministering while under judgment

God always has His chosen representatives and leadership—His ministry order to govern His chosen people and church. We pray, *"May thy Kingdom come on earth,"* then we deny this Christ-given Bible prayer by ignoring His government. God clearly appointed the Levitical priesthood (Num. 17:1–3). The Rod of Aaron, the head of the tribe of Levi, was chosen. Now, the act of not being obedient to God's chosen appointed callings and leadership is a rebellion that most people walk in. Seek out God's government: *"And we beseech you, brethren, to know them which labor among you, and are over you in the Lord, and admonish you"* (1 Thess. 5:12).

We see the rebellion to Christ-given authority placement in the dealings of Korah, a Levi descendant and priest (Lev. 16:9). He and his company demanded equal recognition to God's choosing of Moses and Aaron. We also have many Korah's today:

> *"Korah, the son of Izhar, the son of Kohath, the son of Levi, and Dathan and Abiram, the sons of Eliab, and On, the son of Peleth, sons of Reuben, took men: And they rose up before Moses, with certain of the children of Israel, two hundred and fifty princes of the assembly, famous in the congregation, men of renown: And they gathered themselves together against Moses and against Aaron, and said unto them, Ye take too much upon you, seeing all the congregation are holy, every one of them, and the LORD is*

*among them: wherefore then lift ye up yourselves above the con-
gregation of the LORD? And when Moses heard it, he fell upon his
face".* (Num. 16:1–4).

When the rebellious deny God's holy placement of you in your ministry calling by coming against you, follow this example of *"he fell upon his
face."* Then, the results will become God's dealings with the rebellious as
he leads us to act and speak: *"And the earth opened her mouth, and swallowed them up, and their houses, and all the men that appertained unto
Korah, and all their goods. They, and all that appertained to them, went
down alive into the pit, and the earth closed upon them: and they perished
from among the congregation"* (Num. 16:32–33).

Likewise today, God has placed leadership among the called eldership. The church will not be what it should be until with repentance we
acknowledgement His ministry giving.

CHAPTER FIVE:

Gideon, God's Chosen Reformer

It takes a reformer's understanding and a warrior's attitude to bring fivefold truths into reality. We need Gideon's warrior spirit today, as the angel of the Lord visited him, and not others: **"The angel of the LORD appeared unto him, and said unto him, The LORD is with thee, thou mighty man of valor"** (Judg. 6:12). Gideon had not yet done what the Lord was going to require of him, but God saw Gideon had the right heart, the needed inner man, the required spirit. He placed himself at risk. God honored the warrior Gideon's spirit, the determination to withstand the threat of enemy bondage forces. Gideon knew the risk and potential enemy backlash to his hidden food project. Regardless of the cost, he acted while his heart was seeking answers from God. His unquestioning obedience is the key to breaking bondages!

This is much like what Abraham demonstrated. He sought God and declined the idolatrous beliefs of his ancestors. That is what true reformers do. They see the untruth and error of customs and the traditions of the elders, then they make every possible effort to bring change. The Lord asked Abraham to leave his people. Immediately, he did so. This is the heart commitment required for change to take place! God sees our obedience and acts accordingly.

Consider this: how does the Lord see you and I? He sees our desire and focus. *"For the eyes of the LORD run to and fro throughout the whole earth, to show himself strong in the behalf of them whose heart is perfect toward him"* (2 Chron. 16:9).

God Responded to Gideon

Why Gideon? Gideon struggled with the question of why; may we do likewise. Why did the circumstances Israel was involved in exist? This exact question needs to be asked to bring answers to what now exists. His first question to the angel exposed this thought of WHY?

Our real observation and issue in this Bible record is: are we like Gideon? Do we struggle with the question of what we see in the church world of today? Are we, as Gideon, asking for answers to our dilemma? Do we likewise ask and struggle with why the church is powerless? Do we question why we greatly differ from what we read about in the Book of Acts? Know this! God will send His angel and meet with those who seek an answer to such questions!

The Lord (honor of honors) visited Gideon, advising him that he would be used to save Israel. Do we see this possibility in ourselves? Why would the Lord visit us in like manner?

Gideon responded with, *"Oh my Lord, wherewith shall I save Israel? behold, my family is poor in Manasseh, and I am the least in my father's house"* (Judg. 6:15). Like most of us, Gideon immediately looked at his natural limitations. The task the Lord requires of us will always be larger than our limitations and humanity. This should bring us to our knees to see that *"without Him, we can do nothing"* (John 15:5). We can be used of God "if" we seek Him for our strength and needs in the battle. "If" is the largest conditional word in the Bible. Are we limited as we see the needs of the world and church, but find ourselves to be incapable of addressing these? This is the time to lean on the Lord with our faith, and then conquer! David, with such a spirit, conquered because he knew the truth: *"And all this assembly shall know that the LORD saves not with sword and spear: for the battle is the LORD'S, and he will give you into our hands"* (1 Sam. 17:47). May this be our faith stance as we face the enemies of untruth! We must know the Lord of hosts; the God of armies is with us as we battle.

The Lord gave this promise to Gideon, and to us, as well. When we determine to stand for His truth and principles in our ministry battles, His promise will be, *"And the LORD said unto him, surely I will be with thee, and thou shall smite the Midianites as one man"* (Judg. 6:16).

Preparation Truths to Victory

This is the type of faith, knowledge, and spirit we need to establish a "five-fold church." We then observe Gideon's obedience being tested. Do we fear God, or do we fear man? This test involved a willingness to tear down what was wrong before God, and it was in direct opposition to family and neighbors—those whom he loved. We risk our self-image as we are called of God to defy wrong beliefs. We make ourselves vulnerable to their displeasure with potential painful results. As it reads in Judges:

> *"The same night, that the LORD said unto him, "Take thy father's young bullock, even the second bullock of seven years old, and throw down the altar of Baal that thy father hath, and cut down the grove that is by it: And build an altar unto the LORD thy God upon the top of this rock, in the ordered place, and take the second bullock, and offer a burnt sacrifice with the wood of the grove which you shall cut down".* (Judg. 6:25)

This is a difficult challenge. To see the tremendous victories God wrought by Gideon, WE must stand against and destroy surrounding false altars, idol groves, and wrong customs. WE will also have to sacrifice our self-image and face the critique and displeasure of those who build false groves and altars.

Other churches may not understand what we are focused on doing, but just do it. Build up the people the Lord has given us with the correct fivefold knowledge and principles. Build as if no one but God is watching. Our destruction of the false must precede any establishing of godly truth. With holy purpose, we must pursue the Godly building. We must count the cost and know that it will involve transgressing the customs of the elders and bring opposition.

Note that the sacrifice of the bullock was made by burning the instruments that produced falsehood in worship; this applies now. This is the first step to gaining victory. Heaven cheers.

Obedience to God and His Word will always defy religious wrongs and normalcies. This will always cause offense to the established unseeing. The test in our overcoming is to break from wrong, accepted norms. This requires a godly focus. The question and real test is: do we please man or obey Christ? We must sacrifice and put to death common paths that differ from His. Building fivefold churches demands breaking from what commonly exists. This does not mean we do not love or have patience with born-of-the-Spirit churches. We pray for and honor them. However, we must be resolute in our pursuit of Christ's revealed truth.

Holy Change and Gideon's Confronting of Traditions

The reformer task will always involve tearing down what needs to be torn down. It is a call to destroy traditions and doctrines when they contradict Bible truth. We are called to *"[cast] down imaginations, and every high thing that exalts itself against the knowledge of God"* (2 Cor. 10:5). Whatever opposes Christ's Lordship *"exalts itself against the knowledge of God"*; this is what must be destroyed. We pray, *"May thy Kingdom come on earth as it is in heaven."* This prayer begins with His Kingdom authority and order in His church!

Our obedience by establishing fivefold ministry will raise skepticism; questions from Pharisees, who do not understand: *"Why do thy disciples transgress the tradition of the elders? for they wash not their hands when they eat bread."* Our Lord answered them by confronting the real issue: *"But he answered and said unto them, Why do ye also transgress the commandment of God by your tradition?"* (Matt. 15:2) Christ's answer must be our answer as we confront Pharisees who cling to traditions of men.

Truth restoration will always involve confrontation; this results in the displeasure of religious Sanballat- and Tobias-like *people*, who defy the truths the godly seek. Be willing to pay the price of man's disapproval; that is true worship as we seek to make Christ Lord. They abused and placed the Apostle Paul in chains for being a reformer and standing for truth. Our Lord never backed down from confronting the Pharisees. They crucified Him. He knew this would happen. Jesus told His followers several times of this coming event. Paul, under God-given anointing, wrote: *"Persecutions, afflictions, which came unto me at Antioch, at Iconium, at Lystra; what persecutions I endured: but out of them all the Lord delivered me. Yea, and all that will live godly in Christ Jesus shall suffer persecution*" (2 Tim. 3:11–12). To build a fivefold church, we will also face persecution. No reformer exists who did not face this. Rejoice in this honor, as we serve the Lord. However, avoid a persecution complex. Nehemiah and Zerubbabel were mocked by Sanballat and Tobias. They mocked the rebuilding of the temple (Neh. 4:1) In time they overcame in their building. The carnal will always mock the spiritual. Know what Paul said: *"out of them all the Lord delivered me."* (2 Tim. 3:11)

God blessed Nehemiah, Zerubbabel, and all kings who restored truth. Be encouraged when others do not understand. Our Lord taught *"if any man serve me, let him follow me; and where I am, there shall also my servant be: if any man serve me, him will my Father honor"* (John 12:26). Following scriptures that others ignore and deny will take a denied self-image and self-life. This is our challenge. Do this, and expect the honoring of the Lord (Ps. 91:14).

Those attending Stephen's stoning saw a natural, destructive death. Spiritual eyes saw Jesus, who is scripturally seated, standing up in applause (Heb. 12:2; Acts 7:56). Lord, grant us spiritual eyes. *"Take up your cross"* was a direction given to Christ's disciples (Mark 8:34): *"And when he had called the people unto him with his disciples also, he said unto them, Whosoever will come after me, let him deny himself, and take up his cross, and follow me."* FIVEFOLD churches are built by people with this mentality! Determine whose servants we are. We either bow to Christ, or to man. Radical Christ obedience and Lordship will bring us to building a fivefold church!

Gideon's Victory, Faith, and Obedience

Gideon was obedient to what he was shown at the Lord's direction:

> *"Then Gideon took ten men of his servants, and did as the LORD had said unto him: and so it was, because he feared his father's household, and the men of the city, that he could not do it by day, that he did it by night. And when the men of the city arose early in the morning, behold, the altar of Baal was cast down, and the grove was cut down that was by it, and the second bullock was offered upon the altar that was built"."* (Judg. 6:27–28)

Why "by night"? Because, by wisdom, he avoided daytime confrontation and provoking an immediate battle. Use wisdom; while others sleep, just DO IT. Those ministries who are satisfied with the status quo of churches will not be looking for answers to this malady. The humbly seeking will find and obey God's Word and remedies.

Others may not see why or what we are doing to establish godly truth, BUT they will see the results. A Gideon-spirited ministry—along with a fervent zeal that conforms to what the Holy Scriptures present—will have results. This victory will bring about the releasing of the captivity of the people! (Isa. 61:1) Scriptures portray what we should now be seeing. Christ and His giving have not changed. After our Lord instructed His disciples with knowledge, He ended with, *"But that the world may know that I love the Father; and as the Father gave me commandment, even so I do"* (John 14:31). We must do likewise! Arise; establish His giving, government, and will.

CHAPTER SIX:
Building by Apostle Christ's Example

Christ Jesus, Our Apostle, Exemplified How to Build

Our Lord is the embodiment of all five callings. Apostle Paul said, *"Consider the Apostle and High Priest of our profession, Christ Jesus"* (Heb. 3:1). We must learn from His example in building. After Christ was baptized by John the Baptist, He spent some time in personal ministry, as written in Matthew, chapter four. He also discerned and chose future apostles. Then He changed His focus and direction in chapter five, when He began to build His fivefold church by training His apostles and His followers in ministry matters.

Christ then formed this disciple company into an army with differing ministry leadership strengths. Moses also exemplified this as he led: *"So I took the chief of your tribes, wise men, and known, and made them heads over you, captains over thousands, and captains over hundreds, and captains over fifties, and captains over tens, and officers among your tribes"* (Duet. 1:15).

Matthew, chapter five truths: In the ministry training of the army, I find no greater example then what is found in Matthew, chapter five. There, we find what Christ Jesus did in response to what He saw. He did four specific, differing things. He began by focusing on those who followed Him: *"And seeing the multitudes, he went up into a mountain: and when he was set, his disciples came unto him: And he opened his mouth, and taught them"* (Matt. 5:1).

Most Bibles entitle these popular scripture writings the "Beatitudes." This "man's" insertion skews and greatly limits the focus. If I were to entitle these scriptures, I would term them "Christ teaching church building"; *"I will build my church"* (Matt. 16:18). This scriptural teaching portrays a much larger scope of understanding than the Beatitudes, which is only one segment of a four-part sermon. As we read through this chapter, we find four strong themes. To summarize:

1. The first is how Jesus reacted upon seeing the multitude. In ministry, we must also first see the "multitudes." Our seeing must provoke action. Ministry and church building deal with people's greatest need: their salvation. Religion never solved anything. Salvation by Christ—who is the door, the way, truth, and life—is the opening of the portal of remedy for every need. Our holy fear of the Lord is the beginning of wisdom. Salvation being brought to the soul of men brings new Kingdom wealth in spirit, soul, and body. Do we see souls in torment that we, by God's grace, are delivered from? Do we see the chasm that separated the rich man from poor Lazarus? Do we love Christ and desire His will that all people be saved? Do we love our fellow man enough to warn them of their eternal destiny on the wrong side of the chasm, as described by Jesus Christ in regards to the rich man and Abraham? Do we love our neighbor enough to act?
2. An easily missed point is *"his disciples came unto him"*; then He taught them. So much ministry time is lost by persuading and pulling on those who are not "our" disciples. He did not stay below to convince others to follow Him. He just went and then dealt with the teachable who did follow. Our lesson: do not waste time on those who do not climb the mountain after you. Minister and mature those who do. Invest and sow into "our" disciples. Then expect a harvest.
3. We build correctly when we understand what Jesus did by not continuing His personal ministry focus, as in Mathew chapter four. Instead, upon seeing the multitudes, he purposely climbed up a mountain. His wisdom and purpose was to train the gospel army to deal with the multitude. This is still the case today. We need an army to reach the

world. We must esteem the work of the Holy Spirit within our fellow soldiers as we build His army.

4. Deeply weigh what our teacher, Apostle Christ, addressed His followers with. Note: this included the original disciples and apostles. He taught them a four-part progressive teaching, which occurs in a specific order. This was discipleship and ministry school class number one. This training brought some who followed Him all the way to the Pentecost's upper room. A summary of His Matthew five teachings is as follows:

Lesson one: Renew your character! Achieve this renewal through repentance. Our new character and the attitude to have, as godly disciples and ministry. This includes all the "attitude-to-be" teachings.

Lesson two: Be prepared for the persecution that will arise when you stand strong in your renewed character and godly life. Be encouraged to be strong in the face of opposition. Prepare your following for the coming battles, when the winds of adversity will blow.

Lesson three: Know that your salvation triggers allegiance to Christ. Stand in your Christ-expected call to minister. This applies to all believers. All are to be light and salt without shame.

Lesson four: Gain continual knowledge. Grow in God, His Word, wisdom, and plan of salvation.

Jesus, Our Apostle in Fivefold Church Building

The following four points are Christ's Bible school to his servants.

First: We must see the terrible need of the multitudes, who are separated from God by sin. Acknowledge that religious Christian heathens do not belong to Him. Preach repentance of sin and the need of holiness. Preach how sin leads to a judgment of eternal death and hell. Preach salvation by faith, in the substitutionary atonement of the cross. When we do this, some will follow (Rom. 10:14). This is more than the truth of "Jesus loves you." John the Baptist, Jesus Christ, and Apostle Paul all preached repentance (Matt. 3:1, 4:17; Acts 24:25). Repentance leads us to holiness, without which we will not see God (Heb. 12:14). God is holy and welcomes those desiring holiness.

Second: Christ Jesus taught that those who followed Him the Beatitudes of Matthew 5:3–9. All of them deal with character. All godly character stems from humility and our love towards God and people. He is holy, and holiness must become the passion of a seeking heart. We see the ugliness of sin when we deny our creator God, rather than honoring Him for who He is. We must see the destruction we bring to others when we breach any perfection of love through our actions. This leads us to understand what David said: *"Worship the Lord in the beauty of holiness."* (Ps. 96:9). If holiness is not beautiful in our sight, we will not understand God. He is holy. All sin is unholy.

Blessed are the humble of spirit as they allow God to arise in their lives. Those who mourn do so because they see the unrighteousness. The humble will dethrone themselves to let our Holy God reign. They will receive the result of His promises. Those who now hunger for righteousness in this world are merciful and gracious. They will receive like mercy. Our God discerns those who are pure of heart with no guile, just as Jesus saw in Nathaniel under a fig tree. Just like God, the peacemakers desire peace with all. He sent Christ Jesus, the Prince of Peace, our Shiloh, who brings us peace as we receive Him (Gen. 49:10; John 14:27).

Our saving faith must always be added to with virtue—that, or die while being fruitless.

God always deals with character first. Without becoming a renewed man, knowledge becomes pig food to the world. We see this truth as a priority message by Apostle Peter: *"Giving all diligence, add to your faith virtue; and to virtue knowledge"* (2 Pet. 1:5). Virtue is the first strength to add. This deals with our character and godliness" (Matt. 5:3–9). Then we are admonished to gain knowledge. Our hearts and character must be our initial focus, to be of spiritual usefulness to God. The first step in church building, strongly teach holiness.

Third: Be aware. Be prepared for the result of walking with renewed character. Years ago, I personally lost friends due to no longer joining them in what we had pursued in common. Some accusations of being judgmental and self-righteous came my way with anger. This was painful in the early stages of my renewed walk and focus. My heart was to love my friends and family. It took several years to gain back what I had lost. Many of them are now saved. Halleluiah!

Often our unsaved friends feel unjustly critiqued by us. They become convicted as we portray a godly life while trying to love them. The Apostle Peter said, *"If ye be reproached for the name of Christ, happy are ye; for the spirit of glory and of God rests upon you: on their part he is evil spoken of, but on your part he is glorified"* (1 Pet. 4:14).

Christ taught persecution will follow us when we pursue a godly life, with a renewed character. This cautioning awareness is much needed. Darkness will not always appreciate the light we now choose to walk in.

Many turn back, because *"he that received the seed into stony places, the same is he that hears the word, and anon with joy receives it; Yet hath he not root in himself, but endures for a while: for when tribulation or persecution arises because of the word, by and by he is offended"* (Matt. 13:20–21). These newly saved souls allowed the washing of the Word to take effect. Their new faith was weak; they lacked roots. They did not stand when the heat of resistance came. *"But call to remembrance the former days, in which, after ye were illuminated, ye endured a great fight of afflictions"* (Heb. 10:32). Some will stand and some will not, as they will fall away, loving Egypt (Heb. 6:6).

As our Lord warned us, persecution will always arise when we change our lives due to the Word. Our Savior in holy wisdom prepared His servants for this. Those who preach a belief of "just receive Jesus and life will be a bed of roses" fail and limit the needed message. A fivefold ministry church will balance the truth. When we preach holiness, Godly fear, and eternal judgment, fewer people will struggle, because they will grow truth roots. They will endure longer than *"a while"* (Matt. 13:21).

When new believers are warned to be cautious in the battle of standing as they pursue holiness and faith, more will stand in their renewed walk. We walk in a darkened world. The unsaved do not want to deal with sin exposure. They will hate you, because they love sin (John 3:19). Ministry training and church building must not ignore this teaching; our Lord taught this as a necessary knowledge for all disciples who followed Him up the mountain.

Fourth: Ministry is for all disciples. The teaching of how to build a fivefold church is learned from what our Lord exemplified. This started with a character focus, and then it progressed. Persecution awareness—rather than a "poor me" focus—is needed in our new faith and ministry expectations.

All disciples who followed Him up the mountain, as well as the first apostles, were taught to know who they were and what they were called to be. Ministry is reflecting what Christ is:

> *"Ye are the salt of the earth: but if the salt have lost his savor, wherewith shall it be salted? it is thenceforth good for nothing, but to be cast out, and to be trodden under foot of men. Ye are the light of the world. A city that is set on a hill cannot be hid. Neither do men light a candle, and put it under a bushel, but on a candlestick; and it giveth light unto all that are in the house. Let your light so shine before men, that they may see your good works, and glorify your Father which is in heaven".* (Matt. 5:13)

Salt cleanses and preserves. Light exposes what darkness hides. Many people are like a cat that does not want to be bathed. We preach and live the message. We either become His ambassadors, or we do not: *"For whosoever shall be ashamed of me and of my words, of him shall the Son of man be ashamed, when he shall come in his own glory, and in his Father's, and of the holy angels"* (Luke 9:26). Our love can be seen by what we do. Always be open to a reality check in regards to your love for Him. His focus is salvation. He sees our ministry walk.

Jesus spoke of dying love: *"Nevertheless I have somewhat against thee, because thou hast left thy first love. Remember therefore from whence thou art fallen, and repent, and do the first works; or else I will come unto thee quickly, and will remove thy candlestick out of his place, except thou repent"*

(Rev. 2:4–5). The "first work" is to repent from sin. "Removed candlestick" refers to people and churches who have lost their light because they did not repent with a renewed love for Christ. Do we love Him and holiness, or want fire insurance?

Notice that after Christ addressed our need to be a "light" ministry, He then followed this with imparting knowledge. Even a baby Christian has the ability to lead someone to Him. Everybody should have a testimony of peace and joy by receiving Christ. All believers should continually grow in knowledge in order to be effective in ministry.

The first knowledge impartation that Jesus dealt with is holiness. We will not know God unless we understand holiness. Repentance is our turning to holiness. Jesus taught us the difference between an impossible righteousness by the law which we are incapable of keeping, and faith without our works. Yet faith is proven to be real by our works. Apostle Paul explains that this latter law leads us to our need of Christ, where we are justified by faith in Him: *"Wherefore the law was our schoolmaster to bring us unto Christ, that we might be justified by faith"* (Gal. 3:24). Jesus taught His disciples that by simply keeping the law, we will not be justified. Jesus taught what the Pharisees missed: *"For I say unto you, That except your righteousness shall exceed the righteousness of the scribes and Pharisees, ye shall in no case enter into the kingdom of heaven"* (Matt. 5:20). Our faith in Christ, the cross and what he personally did for us through His substitutionary atonement exceeds our work of law-keeping. Faith is in Him, and the cross; this makes us righteous in God's sight; none are righteous without it. God is the judge of all the earth, and He gives us imputed holiness. In addition, He demands that we pursue a walk of personal holiness.

CHAPTER SEVEN:
Maturing the Fivefold Church

Key Truth: Maturing Elders

We often wish the Lord would send us some mature elders to join us in our ministry vision; this prayer is rarely answered. The truth is, we need to rise up and mature the elders in our churches. We can do so by spending a minimum of one night a week with them in a leadership training program. During this time, we can share teachings of doctrine through conversation. Discuss the ministry needs of our flock, and teach temperance, humility, Fruit of the Spirit, wisdom, and ministry principles. We can also plan how leadership can be released and involved in practical ministry. Ordained elders will come from these interactions, where there is a teachable spirit. If no stronger teaching materials are available, I suggest going through our "Fivefold Church Doctrinal Manual," a forty-two-doctrinal teaching manual that includes the foundational doctrines (see back of book).

The Baby-Sit Church

The same principles of teaching and personal interaction apply to maturing the committed church adherents. Be honest! Before describing the five given callings, and then giving some examples of error and failure in our ministries, let us deal with the critical reality of current church dealings with the believer body. Most ministries have a wrong expectation of the believer body and their maturity—this is what their ministry focus should be. Most churches have a expectation of "baby-sitting" from their assembly. This may seem to be a hard and uncharitable assessment, but

Bible facts speak. I love the church and our Lord Jesus enough to challenge the status quo that exists. Change is needed.

Bible-Written Critiques of "Baby Status"

With love for the church and for Christ Jesus our Lord, as all should have, we want the church to be what it should be. It is painful to place this critique under a scriptural microscope.

The Hebrew church should have been the most mature church. They had the Jewish background of Patriarchs and covenants. Paul wanted to share deeper scriptural subject matter with them, such as understanding the Melchizedek priesthood. Few ministries share Melchizedek truth and deeper subject matter; even if they did, most of their hearers would not grasp these truth topics.

Preachers who wait on the Lord will receive the Bible's truth revelations. When they share these truths, they wonder why they do not "stick"; when they are not readily received, the preachers walk away with the thought of I failed in my presentation. Or they think that the people are dull in their understanding. The truth is that the preachers are dull in understanding. They have not taught the foundational doctrines. The people are not capable of grasping deeper revelation truths unless they have a thorough understanding of these doctrines; after all, elementary school precedes our learning of college-level material.

Paul discerned that he could not teach deeper subject matter. He explains why, as he correctly calls the people immature babies:

*"Called of God a high priest after the order of Melchizedec. Of whom we have many things to say, and hard to be uttered, seeing ye are dull of hearing. For when for the time ye ought to be teachers, ye have need that one teach you again which be the first principles of the oracles of God; and are become such as have need of milk, and not of strong meat. For every one that uses milk is unskillful in the word of righteousness: for **he is a babe**. But strong meat belongs to them that are of full age, even those who by reason of use have their senses exercised to discern good and evil".* (Heb. 5:10)

He further outlined how we can gain the needed course for correction—that is, the people's maturity that would enable them to absorb deeper truths. Paul outlined the six basic foundational doctrines of the Christian church: *"Therefore leaving the principles of the doctrine of Christ, let us go on unto perfection* [maturity]; *not laying again the foundation of repentance from dead works, and of faith toward God, Of the doctrine of baptisms, and of laying on of hands, and of resurrection of the dead, and of eternal judgment"* (Heb. 6:1–2). Either we are ignorant of the need to understand these doctrines, or WE ARE WISER THAN GOD. Do not ignore thoroughly teaching these doctrines. Without our people understanding these doctrines, they will be a continual babysitting project. It takes time to teach these, but there will be a momentous change when our flock is mature and capable of giving a minor teaching of them. This is part of ministry responsibility—the maturing of fivefold saints.

The early church after Pentecost experienced an explosion in growth. We need to understand why this was and follow what they did. They had a church setting that we do not uphold today! Of the nine "and" words listed (Acts 2:42–47), note the first "and": *"And they continued steadfastly in the apostles' doctrine and fellowship."* These doctrinally equipped saints had the ministry success we read about in letters to the churches.

"And fellowship": this means that the church had spiritual family, loving friendship, and times of communication. This was not a Sunday morning schedule; this was spending evenings together to discuss faith and doctrine. Where are the people who seek proven, accepted, and genuine apostles? All mature and called apostles will naturally teach doctrine (just as birds sing).

Ask 99 percent of the church what these doctrines are, and you will see a deer caught in the headlights. The painful truth is that when asked, 99 percent of the church-named elders cannot even name these six basic foundational doctrines. When asked to give a minor teaching on each of these doctrines, they become embarrassed. Therefore, most churches, according to Apostle Paul, *"are become such as have need of milk, and not of strong meat"* (Heb. 5:12). I personally accuse most churches of this dilemma.

Is this not true? Even after attending church for years, do most named Christians not *"need that one teach you again, which be the first principles of the oracles of God" (Heb. 5:12)*? Be honest! Paul taught what a reasonable expectation of believers is: *"For when for the time ye ought to be teachers"* (Heb. 5:12). This is the Bible's expectation standard; this is the road to gaining scriptural maturity. Lord, help us bring change to this, by teaching these *"first principles"*—the doctrines of our Christian faith (Heb. 6:1-2). Hold a recurring Bible doctrine study one evening a week. Doing so will bring people the maturity they need with basic doctrinal knowledge. This applies to maturing our new and old saints, as well.

This sad assessment is a common church reality. If they had a "mature" apostle headship, this would not be the case. Apostle Paul always taught and admonished growing apostles to focus on teaching doctrine: *"Preach the word; be instant in season, out of season; reprove, rebuke, exhort with all longsuffering and doctrine. For the time will come when they will not endure sound doctrine; but after their own lusts shall they heap to themselves teachers, having itching ears"* (2 Tim. 4:2–3). This *"time"* and these *"itching ears"* are upon us here and now with "itching-ears preachers!"

The elders and ministry are to be blamed for this. By our discerning genuine apostles and teachers, and by maturing our ministering elders, our churches will change. Doctrinal topics are more of a natural part of the wiring of the apostle's burden. Teachers will expound these truths more than evangelists and prophets. Some upon reading this will feel demeaned and quit reading this writing. Others will repent and seek to change and establish truth. The humble and repentant will bring change by upholding fivefold ministry doctrinal truths!

The first doctrine deals with repentance, and what work leads to death. This is the separation of moral light and darkness. This is a separation of roads. Whether the roads lead to life or to death.

The second doctrine deals with our faith in God: who God is, the deity of Christ, and the person of the Holy Spirit. It is the doctrine of the Trinity and the four attributes of God, including holiness.

The third doctrine deals with the three distinct New Testament baptisms, defined by who does the baptizing, what someone is baptized into, and when the baptism happens. Ministry anointing is increased, and as a result. Scriptural Bible Christians seek to experience being genuinely baptized in the Spirit. The gifts (not the Fruit) of the Spirit are a result. Normal and newly "baptized-in-the-Spirit" believers all experience at least one of the gifts of the Spirit.

The fifth doctrine deals with the two separate resurrections of the dead. When do these happen? Why are people separated, and why do they experience the two separate resurrections?

The sixth doctrine deals with the two separate and eternal judgments of all. Both saved and unsaved people will all be judged at differing times based upon their works. They both receive eternal rewards. The damned are also individually rewarded with eternal consequences.

Ministry must also teach our people about Fruit of the Spirit, gifts of the Spirit, gospel armor, etc. Our ministry has an inexpensive nine-doctrine manual that extensively covers the foundational doctrines. We also have a longer forty-two-doctrine truths manual ("Fivefold Churches Doctrinal Manual"), available for the elder and mature believer's ministry.

Teaching the Foundational Doctrines

These doctrines are a treasure of understanding. They bring strength; assurance and joy.

First doctrine: *"of repentance from dead works."* (Heb. 6:1) Ask and teach this doctrine by giving multiple scriptures that will textually provide the answers. An open discussion with questions and answers is effective. Ask the following:
a)   Why is this the first doctrine to learn?
b)   What is repentance, and how long do we experience repentance?
c)   Why repent from "dead works" and not sin?
d)   What is our responsibility in sanctification? (1 Thess. 4:3)
e)   What is the result of repentance?

Second doctrine: *"of faith toward God."* Ask and teach:
a)   What is the faith that God requires?
b)   What are the four attributes of God?
c)   If we are saved, why does God demand holiness from us?

d) Is there one God? Explain the doctrine of the Trinity.

e) How is Jesus Christ both God and man?

f) Is the Holy Spirit God?

g) How is Jesus God, man, and the Father all at once? (Isa. 9:6)

Third doctrine: *"the doctrine of baptisms."* Ask and teach:

a) Who does the baptizing? What into?

b) When do these three New Testament baptisms take place?

c) Why is the 1 Cor. 12:13 baptism the first baptism?

d) How does this baptism relate to experiencing being born again?

e) Why does God require water baptism, and when?

f) Why does Rom. 6:4 say "buried" in baptism?

g) What is the difference between being born of the Spirit and baptized in the Spirit?

h) How does one receive this baptism in the Spirit?

i) What are the gifts of the Spirit versus the Fruit of the Spirit?

Fourth doctrine: *"laying on of hands."* Ask and teach:

a) What is the symbolism of "laying on of hands"?

b) Does this apply to all believers in the ministry?

c) Do we need to get "ordained" after an education in order to exercise and have this functioning?

d) Do we expect results when exercising this in our ministry, when we have not experienced the "baptism of the Holy Spirit"? What brings a stronger response of the Holy Spirit in some ministries, when compared to others? Is God prejudiced?

Fifth doctrine: *"resurrection of the dead."* Ask and teach:

a) How many times is there a resurrection of the dead?

b) How long apart are they and why?

c) Who rises in the first resurrection? Who in the second?

d) What two things does Christ do when He comes again?

e) If the saints are with the Lord after experiencing a physical death, what happens to the saints at the resurrection of the dead?

f) What heavenly signs trigger the first resurrection?

Sixth doctrine: *"eternal judgment."* Ask and teach:
a) Why were the saints judged following the first resurrection?
b) Why were damned souls judged at the second resurrection?
c) What was the basis for not being part of the first resurrection?
d) What eternally happened to the saints in the first resurrection?
e) What happened to the judged in the second resurrection?
f) How long did the lake of fire exist?

Bible example of the scriptural Church

What our Church should be Today

We have examined the normal New Testament church. I don't wish to be repetitive, but due to the huge importance of this truth, again consider Acts, chapter fifteen. There, we see a clear demonstration of how much we have changed from what a church's "normal" should be.

Our existing common views and practices regarding the believer body (in regards to ministry and doctrinal matters) are so limited. Many people incorrectly believe that only "called" ministries who attain Bible school degrees are worthy to minister and be allowed to contribute in church ministry; this is so unscriptural, and it's an existing error that should not be. Attending a Bible school should increase knowledge, but Holy Spirit anointing and the understanding of Bible revelation truths only come through the Holy Spirit. The five called ministries and elders mature the church, enabling believers to contribute in ministry. We must change this wrong expectation. These Bible texts speak to this and say so much:

Ministry, believer church functions exemplified; why not today?

"And when they were come to Jerusalem, they were received of the church, and of the apostles and elders, and they declared all things that God had done with them." They accepted and honored out-of-town ministries. They *"were received of the church, and of the apostles"* (Acts 15:4). Now we have a strong separation within *the church,* between laity, and the ministry, along with few discerned mature *apostles.* Today, guest ministries are usually received by the pastor. We must involve the church with a

different expectation of believers. We must honor and uphold them as a functional ministering body.

a) *"Then all the multitude kept silence, and gave audience to Barnabas and Paul, declaring what miracles and wonders God had wrought among the Gentiles by them"* (Acts 15:12). This was at the gathering of the "church." All attended discussions of serious doctrinal matters; *"the multitude"* were present and party to this discussion. Today, this would be limited to the apostle, the pastor, and maybe an elder's discussion. In the New Testament church, everyone took part in and approved the elder's verdict. Everyone should discuss doctrine to become of "one mind." This is mostly avoided today (1 Cor. 1:10).

b) *"Then pleased it the apostles and elders, with the whole church, to send chosen men of their own company to Antioch with Paul and Barnabas; namely, Judas surnamed Barsabas, and Silas, chief men among the brethren"* (Acts 15:22). It pleased the leadership elders and *"the whole church, to send chosen men."* Today, *"the whole church"* is not involved in—nor do they speak to—the conclusion of such matters. Our Holy Bible examples are ignored. Genuine and mature fivefold churches will bring change to the maturing of and expectation of the body. Currently, we have this prideful and demeaning separation of laity and clergy.

c) *"And they wrote letters by them after this manner; The apostles and elders and brethren send greeting unto the brethren which are of the Gentiles in Antioch and Syria and Cilicia"* (Acts 15:23). This decision made was documented and sent out by *"The apostles and elders and brethren."* Today, due to the clergy and laity wall, only clergy will be dealing with this decision and the sending. We keep our babies in the nursery by this type of inaction. This may sound a little facetious, but this painful truth cannot be denied!

d) *"So when they were dismissed, they came to Antioch: and when they had gathered the multitude together, they delivered the epistle"* (Acts 15:30). The Antioch church demonstrated the same believer maturity expectations as the Jerusalem church. Why do we not, in our church today? In Antioch *"the multitude"* dealt with doctrine. None were regarded as immature. No pre-chewed food was delivered to babies, as everyone was to process truth.

e) *"And Judas and Silas, being prophets also themselves, exhorted the brethren with many words, and confirmed them. And after they had tarried there a space, they were let go in peace from the brethren unto the apostles"* (Acts 15:32–33). This concept, *"they were let go,"* is foreign language to our churches. The elders, who were released *"in peace,"* were mature prophets. Their departure *"from the brethren"* was weighed in unity. There was communication and submission.

Mutual accountability was practiced in releasing the prophets to their next assignment. This letting go *"from the brethren unto the apostles"* involved more than the apostles or elders. We need a different maturity expectation of our "brethren." This will change when we change—when we make the change of having scriptural elders oversee a fivefold church.

Observe; the prophets were released to go to the apostles and not Jerusalem. They upheld correct ministry authority oversight with humility. This may be a little difficult for some to swallow. These scriptural realities are foreign to most of today's mindset. This is so far from what now exists. The day is coming. We will again see genuine fivefold churches where all will strive to function as we read, by following our holy scriptural pattern.

The Responsibility of Called Ministry

We must see a clear setting out of the Christ-given expectations of the five callings. Let us carefully review these scriptures: *"And he gave some, apostles; and some, prophets; and some, evangelists; and some, pastors and teachers; For the perfecting of the saints, for the work of the ministry, for the edifying of the body of Christ"* (Eph. 4:11–12). Our Savior gave these callings with specific explained holy purpose. Not some, but all five callings are given for *"the perfecting of the saints."* "Perfecting" means maturing. All five callings should impart their unique Holy-Spirit ministry wiring, their burden, and their vision strengths.

All five callings are to prepare the saints for their ministry: *"From whom the whole body fitly joined together and compacted by that which every joint supplies, according to the effectual working in the measure of every part, makes increase of the body unto the edifying of itself in love*" (Eph. 4:16). We must teach this expectation and then release the saints. How did these saints achieve such maturity? They fellowshipped with ministry (Acts 2:40).

Make room for the saints. Enable them to express and edify the body by what *"every joint supplies"* (Eph. 4:16). Let them know that you expect them to minister. All the saints are to be matured in vision, knowledge, and heart preparation in order to win and help mature souls. All matured saints are to have their toolbox filled with doctrinal knowledge, gifts, and Fruit of the Spirit. Enable them to minister. All the saints are to be matured in spiritual matters. All of them must strongly understand the baptism of the Holy Spirit, the revelation, and the resulting gifts. How else can they do the work of the ministry?

Believers should be capable of answering the questions of those they should be ministering to. Fivefold elder are responsible for maturing them. We must equip the church for their ministry! That must be our heart's desire! We were not called to just let others see our glamorous personal ministry. All believers should mature with teaching ability as they reach out in ministry! The multiple eldership has guilt, when they do not help the believers understand, "*For whosoever shall be ashamed of me and of my words, of him shall the Son of man be ashamed, when he shall come in his own glory and in his Father's*" (Lk. 9:26)

The real saints maturity expectation is, "*For indeed because of the time, you ought to be teachers*"! The direction for how to become mature is this this: "*you have need that one teach you again what are the first principles of the oracles of God*" (Heb. 5:11). The maturing of the church by the five callings involves covering the basics first. All should be knowledgeable. All should be capable of giving a teaching on the six foundational doctrines. It is a holy process.

Sadly, the truth is that we have named Bible scholars and Bible schools with graduates who don't have this knowledge ability. Many of these people pervert scriptures and deny the baptism of the Holy Spirit and the giving of five separate ministry callings. Practically all churches deny the New Testament Christ-given authority order at this time. Most still teach that the original twelve apostles are all that there is, while ignoring apostles Paul, Barnabas, Timothy, etc., and those who are Christ-given today (Acts 14:14; 1 Thess. 1:1, 2:6).

CHAPTER EIGHT:
God's Heart, Omniscient Plan

Our Christian ministry: We are to reveal God's heart, His desire for His saints now and in eternity. God reveals His eternal salvation plan to His called ministry. First, this revelation illuminates the sin gap between God and man, as well as His remedy by the cross. Should this not be true, then we are not called to a fivefold calling—only to being religious peddlers, instead. God, due to being omniscient and knowing all things from eternity past to eternity future, planned salvation to be possible. Omniscience is an ability that we read about but do not relate to, as this is beyond us; for now (1 Co. 13:12).

God's omniscience is proven by the prophetic foreknowledge in Bible writings. We do not understand this God ability any more than how the world and sun maintain their orbit with a perfect-distance relationship. Our world and life would perish without this exactness.

By His omniscience, God knew man would fall into sin. By His love, He knowingly planned salvation, the remedy for sin, before the world was created. Our Christian salvation differs from all other world religions. Our faith lies in receiving substitutionary atonement for sin. Christ paid our penalty for sin, our deserved death by His crucifixion. All other religions have a self-goodness perfection by works belief. Saved Christians know that our good works do not save us. Born-of-the-Spirit Christians believe Christ's death is full payment for our sins.

The devil gained power over the death of man when man accepted his lying temptation. He enticed man to become as God (Gen. 3:4, 15; Heb. 2:14). God foreknew man's choice (Gen. 3:6). God revealed salvation's plan immediately after man's fall. The seed of the woman (Christ) would crush Satan's head (Gen. 3:15; Gal. 3:16). Jesus—the Messiah born as a holy, sinless man—faced death, the penalty for our guilt. Our deserved spiritual death and eternal separation from our God was cancelled due to what Christ did in our stead.

We became unholy due to having breached the perfection of love, the holiness that God is. Those who repent of sin and believe in God's love by Christ will receive forgiveness. This born-in-the-manger child is also the eternal God and Father. This mystery is much too difficult for any human mind. Isaiah writes that the child who is born is the Son who is given, and also the everlasting Father (Isa. 9:6). Apostle Paul acknowledges the mystery of this fact (1 Tim. 3:16).

In this scriptural passage, Isaiah also reveals the government of Christ: *"For unto us a child is born, unto us a son is given: and the government shall be upon his shoulder"* (Isa. 9:6). Christ Jesus is no longer the baby in the manger. Now, our Jesus is Lord of all (Acts 2:36).

We gain fivefold ministry church building strength when we understand Christ's plan. He is the eternal Lord of the church (Eph. 5:23). Our LORD of the church has given what He says we need: His five given ministry callings in His government. When we deny and disregard Christ's fivefold giving and authority order, we deny Him and His Lordship!

Omniscience

We must see and accept God's omniscience, even when we do not understand it. Omniscience is a major factor in ministry building and church building. Seeing the truth of omniscience reveals God, His heart, and His plan. By God's omniscience, He foreknew all people. This includes their decisions and actions, from Adam to the last soul. He knew this before the world was created. Our God is God!

He is omnipresent, being everywhere in the universe. He is omnipotent, being all-powerful and with limitless ability, as demonstrated when He spoke the universe into being at creation. By Christ, He holds the universe in place (Heb. 1:3). Omniscience is God knowing all things past, present, and future all at once. Bible prophecy is due to God's omniscience, as seen by His foretelling of coming events.

God created us in His image. With our free will, He allows us to choose our actions, He also holds us responsible for them. Man must respond to God's appeal. We are to seek. God's Word says that even if no man preached, the heavens and earth are His sermon (Ps. 19:1–3).

Job and Abraham responded to this sermon. They sought God, and He was found by them. They sought Him and His righteousness while forsaking the heathen heritage of their forefathers. Just as these tremendous men forsook what was wrong and embraced righteousness, our building of God's New Testament fivefold church is also embracing righteousness. We honor God's revelation by His Word. God knows our hearts while we wrestle to make correct decisions. Ministry is when His servants enter the work of Christ's eternal plan of salvation. He knows the results, *"as he hath chosen us in him before the foundation of the world, that we should be holy and without blame before him in love"* (Eph. 1:4). We seek His glory. We worship Him, as we do our part in fulfilling His plan.

With love for Him and our fellow man, in our ministry pursuits we must submit to our Lord's given New Testament building blueprints. These blueprints set out how we are to do our part in establishing His church ministry government. He is our eternal God. Our God declared His being to Moses when He said, "tell Pharaoh that I AM sent you" ("the existing one", Exod. 3:14). Our resurrected Lord Jesus said, *"I AM Alpha and Omega"* (the beginning and the end, Rev. 1:8, 11). Our human minds reel at the thought of omniscience. This is so far beyond our humanity. By accepting this revealed Bible knowledge, we will have less struggles with Christ coming as God, the *"KING of KINGS and LORD of LORDS" (Rev. 19:16).*

Christ is proven to be God, by the *"spirit of prophecy"* (Rev. 19:10). God reveals Himself as the Father, Son, and Holy Spirit: the divine Trinity. He also teaches us that He is one God: *"Hear, O Israel: The LORD our God is one LORD"* (Deut. 6:4). The church is taught, *"For there are three that bear record in heaven, the Father, the Word, and the Holy Ghost: and these three are one"* (1 John 5:7). Paul the Apostle helps all of us when he said, *"And without controversy great is the mystery of godliness: God was manifest in the flesh, justified in the Spirit, seen of angels, preached unto the Gentiles"* (1 Tim. 3:16).

The Qur'an—or cult writings—do not demonstrate prophecy when we compare them to the Bible. The Holy Spirit is the author of Bible prophecy. Bible-written prophetic truths were written by holy men of old as the Holy Ghost moved upon them (2 Pet. 1:21). Foreknowledge expressed by Prophecy is hard evidence of God, Christ as God, and the Holy Bible; no rational mind can deny this. Weigh the following scriptures—which are only a few of the many scriptures available—that were written from two thousand to four thousand years ago:

1. *"And I fell at his feet to worship him. And he said unto me, See thou do it not: I am thy fellow servant, and of thy brethren that have the testimony of Jesus:* **worship God: for the testimony of Jesus is the spirit of prophecy**" (Rev. 19:10). Prophecy proves that Christ is Lord and God (John 20:28). Undeniable prophecies prove His person, purposes, and omniscience. The church MUST receive His Lordship. We do so by establishing His church government!

2. Those who struggle with prophetic truths consider this writing of two thousand years ago: *"And he causes all, both small and great, rich and poor, free and bond, to receive a mark in their right hand, or in their foreheads: And that no man might buy or sell, save he that had the mark, or the name of the beast, or the number of his name"* (Rev. 13:16–17). This refers to the coming Antichrist. He is the last world dictator before Christ comes back. His reign ends when he is destroyed at Christ's second coming for His church (2 Thess. 2:8). We now see satellite communication ability's. This makes a one world dictator and a cashless society wih "Krypto currency" possible. Impossible to see in a donkey transportation day. The Bible was mocked when these possibilities seemed to be impossible and ridiculous.

3. An easy-to-verify prophecy—one out of perhaps fifty that specifically speaks of Israel—is the Jews prophesied scattering and then regathering:

   "And I scattered them among the heathen, and they were dispersed through the countries: according to their way and according to their doings I judged them. . . . And I will sanctify my great

name, which was profaned among the heathen, which ye have profaned in the midst of them; and the heathen shall know that I am the LORD, says the Lord GOD, when I shall be sanctified in you before their eyes. For I will take you from among the heathen, and gather you out of all countries, and will bring you into your own land". (Ezek. 36:19, 23–24).

Documented history shows that this prophetic Word, written some 2,700 years ago, has now been fulfilled. The Roman Empire's General Titus attempted to annihilate all Jews in 70 AD. Due to this, they were world scattered. Some 1,900 years later, the "gathering" by Hitler (the hunter) during the Holocaust of World War II took place *"The LORD lives, that brought up the children of Israel from the land of the north [Russia], and from all the lands whither he had driven them: and I will bring them again into their land that I gave unto their fathers. 16 Behold, I will send for many fishers, says the LORD, and they shall fish them; and after will I send for many hunters, and they shall hunt them from every mountain, and from every hill, and out of the holes of the rocks"* (Jer. 16:15–16). They regathered due to escaping from the Jew genocide hunt, and again became a world-recognized nation in 1948.

4. By His omniscience, God knows who will ultimately be saved. God knew this even before the creation of the world: *"For the children being not yet born, neither having done any good or evil, that the purpose of God according to election might stand, not of works, but of him that calls; . . . As it is written, Jacob have I loved, but Esau have I hated"* (Rom. 9:11). God foreknew that Esau would despise holy promise and privilege, such as his birthright.

Calvinistic churches do not understand this truth in their teachings of predestination and election. God judges our every action and thought. He foreknew our choices before the world was created (Rom. 8:29). This is clarified by the following: *"Known unto God are all his works from the beginning of the world"* (Acts 15:18). This scripture explains the salvation of those whom God foreknew. As it reads in Romans, *"For whom he did foreknow, he also did <u>predestinate</u> to be conformed to the image of his Son,* *that he might be the firstborn among many brethren. Moreover whom he did predestinate, them he also called: and whom he called, them he justified: and whom he justified, them he also glorified"* (Rom. 8:29–30).

By God's omniscience, He foreknew our actions and planned salvation for those who would seek Him. We, the believers, are required of God to make our election sure; this is our responsibility. God judges our continual faith as we work out our salvation: *"Wherefore the rather, brethren, give diligence to make your calling and election sure: for if ye do these things, ye shall never fall"* (2 Pet. 1:10; Phil. 2:10, Eph. 2:8; Rev. 2:23). In maintaining our salvation, we have responsibilities.

God declares, *"According as he hath chosen us in him before the foundation of the world, that we should be holy and without blame before him in love"* (Eph. 1:4). Here is the truth of God's salvation plan through Christ, as He uses us to build His church.

Moses' Building

The pursuit and the establishing of genuine fivefold churches is the epitome of endeavors. Our church building is comparable to Moses building the tabernacle in the wilderness, where God met with Israel. The Lord told Moses to build with exact materials, measurements, and colors (Ex. 39:1). Moses was faithful to build as per these holy instructions. The result was that God manifested His presence in this temple. This temple was accurately built following His directions; God's manifested presence was the sure evidence of the obedience Moses exemplified.

Likewise, we will experience God's anointing and manifest presence when we will build as per His plans. Today, this involves our returning, with repentance, to Christ's given and desired ministry government involving the five distinct callings. Christ sets what is mostly ignored in the church today: *"ye are the body of Christ, and members in particular. And God hath set some in the church, first apostles, secondarily prophets, thirdly teachers, after that miracles"* (1 Cor. 12:27–28).

Confront and destroy the lie's many projects. This is not only for a first-church generation: *"Ye are the body of Christ . . . And God hath set some **in the** church."* Seek God's setting!

Writing to the Hebrew church, Paul refers to church building: *"Who serve unto the example and shadow of heavenly things, as Moses was admonished of God when he was about to make the tabernacle: for, See, says he, that thou make all things according to the pattern shewed to thee in the mount"* (Heb. 8:5). In comparison, our Lord and Savior Jesus Christ has given us our heavenly pattern to build His church. Until we build the church according to His given pattern, unlike Moses, we limit church building and the manifestation of the holy presence; the results of ignoring this are seen everywhere.

When we faithfully build as per Christ's holy directions, we, the world, and our enemies will see the result. Generally, we have denied our Lord's given pattern. Then we wonder why we see and experience a vastly different church from what we read about in the holy New Testament! Establishing a FIVEFOLD MINISTRY is our effort to rebuild the church as per our Christ-given pattern. This type of church building demands His ministry servants' accurate obedience to His Word!

CHAPTER NINE:
Servant Heart, Key to Building

A critically important key to building a fivefold church is that all people involved must demonstrate genuine heartfelt servanthood. Real servanthood is a depth of humility to Christ. This is living what Paul teaches in marriage: "*Wives, submit yourselves unto your own husbands, as unto the Lord*" (Eph. 5:22). A servant attitude acknowledges Christ as the Lord of our lives and church.

This will determine the reality of our ministry's focus and building. The prioritization of being servants in our ministry is a must. Egos that deny that we are Christ's given servants always destroy our building. We are taught to "*by love serve one another*" (Gal. 5:13). Our priority in love must be to serve Christ first, then one another. Serving Christ involves projecting His Holy love and Truth.

This will cause us to withstand error while we establish His Bible truths. An example of an error (a "Christian" untruth) that brings death to millions of named Christians is infant baptism. Some people are taught the untruth of having received the Holy Spirit due to this unscriptural rite. This belief denies that we are to personally hear and believe the gospel, in order to be sealed by The Spirit (Eph. 1:13). We must destroy all wrong doctrines. Withstanding untruth will earn us the displeasure of the ignorant. Total obedience to Christ will cause us to experience a Zipporah-type of judgment by those who do not understand: "*It came to pass by the way in the inn, that the LORD met him, and sought to kill him. Then Zipporah took a sharp stone, and cut off the foreskin of her son, and cast it at his feet, and said, surely a bloody husband art thou to me. So he let him go: then she said, A bloody husband thou art, because of the circumci-sion"* (Exod. 4:24–26).

Zipporah looked at the natural with a motherly, protective eye. When dealing with carnal man, it is a challenge to be spiritual. Writings about Christ speak to this: *"He is despised and rejected of men; a man of sorrows, and acquainted with grief"* (Isa. 53:3). We must first count the cost and decide to pay the price of obeying Christ while building His church (Luke 14:28). Do not expect approval from all people; do, however, expect heaven's applause (Acts 7:55).

Obedience When Facing Rejection

Humility involves obedience to God's Lordship. Moses knew what was required, as given by the Abrahamic covenant. When confronted by the Lord, Moses obeyed to do what he already knew to obey: the circum-cision of his son. His reluctance to obey this God-demanded covenant procedure was due to his weakness; he wished to avoid the displeasure of his wife. Zipporah grudgingly complied. The anger Moses had attempted to avoid now came. Our fear of man tempts us to compromise to avoid disapproval. We can only serve one master.

To undertake a great task with holy signs and anointing, as Moses experienced, we must count the cost and overcome in our preparation. Be obedient in fivefold ministry. Our future ministries depend on our obedience to God in the matters of today. Preparation for this involves a death to the god of self. To enthrone Christ means complete obedi-ence while surrendering to God's Word. God demanded circumcision. Likewise, Christ demands that we establish His setting in place of His church government. Servants seek to implement this.

Now, look at the result of Moses' ministry, a named friend of God, what he accomplished. Being focused as a servant of God involves our radical obedience, love, and worship. We must have faith in Him with humility. His Word and wisdom is higher than ours: *"For my thoughts are not your thoughts, neither are your ways my ways, says the LORD"* (Isa. 55:8).

Fivefold Church Obedience

Christ's higher ways need to be followed in order to build fivefold ministry churches. Denominational and independent churches who deny what we term "fivefold truths" are either ignorant, or they are in denial of God's wisdom and building. With their faith in Him, His servants, with wholehearted holy worship, will bring this church reality into being.

As we know, Christ gave ministry gifts to the church: "*And he gave some, apostles; and some, prophets; and some, evangelists; and some, pastors and teachers*" (Eph. 4:11). By not striving to understand how we are to apply this is an unholy rebellion to Christ's Lordship.

This act of Christ's giving includes an appointed authority role, "*God hath set some in the church, first apostles, secondarily prophets, thirdly teachers, after that miracles, then gifts of healings, helps, governments, diversities of tongues*" (1 Cor. 12:28). When we reason away how to understand and implement this setting without servant-hearted humility, we are rebellious to Christ; we are disregarding His Word. All denominational and onefold ministries deny this giving. This is the Bible's order of church governmental authority.

The reformer Martin Luther nailed the truth of "the just shall live by faith" to a church door. He withstood the untruth he had uncovered; may fivefold ministry people do likewise.

Personally, I have seen the field that contains the pearl of great price, and I am selling all to acquire this field (Matt. 13:46). I see the huge damage to the Kingdom that is caused by our denial of this truth. Do not tell me you love Christ and have made Him the Lord of your life and ministry while ignoring these scriptures. Repentance is the first doctrine to apply in salvation and ministry. When we disregard scriptures, we then deny our Lord by doing "our thing." We must trust Christ's Word and wisdom by pursuing the establishment of a fivefold church. Moses was not perfect, but he learned obedience as he became a great man of God. At the end of his journey, the Lord himself buried his body.

As Moses, we must build as per the pattern that was given to us by the Lord who is seated at the right hand of God the Father. The fivefold church ministry and government is the pattern of His holy blueprint that we are to follow. Read and study this pattern in order to build the genuine, New Testament church.

Humility Realities

While we struggle with discerning genuine differing ministry callings, we also wrestle with how we make these callings flow together in the church body. Our intention is to have what Christ our Lord desires. The result will be a church body edifying itself in love with unity, and increase of itself: *"From whom the whole body fitly joined together and compacted by that which every joint supplies, according to the effectual working in the measure of every part, makes increase of the body unto the edifying of itself in love"* (Eph. 4:16).

To achieve this will demand humility, as we deal with doctrine, eldership, finances, and more. In my years of ministry and having offered to make myself available to all, I am always disappointed that I rarely have fellow ministry members be willing to reason with me when disagreeing with any doctrine I present as truth. This includes supposedly mature ministries that attend leadership ministry conferences, which I have been blessed to be involved with.

Such ministry members may have reasons for not dialoging, but whatever they are, they are wrong. These leaders know my ministry, as well as theirs, affect many others. With a love for Christ, my person, and especially those who I potentially reach, they should correct me when they think I am wrong. Many follow a path of supposed peace by silence. How can we have a strong unity in building together when we do not have a unity of mind? We see God Himself presenting this argument to us while dealing with salvation: *"Come now, and let us reason together, says the LORD"* (Isa. 1:18).

Some claim Apostle Paul taught that a Christian "peace ministry" is achieved by accepting others without a discussion of differences in doctrinal subjects.

WRONG: I strongly disagree; that is not scriptural truth. Paul taught the Corinthian church as follows: *"I beseech you, brethren, by the name of our Lord Jesus Christ, that ye all speak the same thing, and that there be no divisions among you; but that ye be perfectly joined together in the same mind and in the same judgment"* (1 Cor. 1:10). To attain unity, we must communicate with a godly humility. Discuss why we differ to become of "one mind?"

As in divorce, undiscussed differences are a root cause for division. Unwillingness to discuss is a subtle pride, and lacks love. Pricilla and Aquila tackled this important subject matter when they met Apollos. They had no hesitation in correcting his baptism beliefs:

> *"And a certain Jew named Apollos, born at Alexandria, an eloquent man, and mighty in the scriptures, came to Ephesus. This man was instructed in the way of the Lord; and being fervent in the spirit, he spoke and taught diligently the things of the Lord, knowing only the baptism of John. And he began to speak boldly in the synagogue: whom when Aquila and Priscilla had heard, they took him unto them, and expounded unto him the way of God more perfectly".* (Acts 18:24–26).

It takes humility and a heart to hear each other out with an open Bible. Many defer from discussing differences by upholding a false peace because they fear rejection. Think of the cost of not speaking out. When we allow a ministry to continue with spreading their wrong doctrine, we allow seeds of death to be sown by them. Where is our love for God, and for the ministry? Do we love the people they will affect in their ministry journey?

The Needed Fivefold Church

The world's harvest fields are overripe. To love Christ means that we love the souls of our fellow man. This is His great love. The early church turned their world upside down. We can turn our world upside down when we will build by God's given government in ministry. We see this possibility presented: *"And when they found them not, they drew Jason and certain brethren unto the rulers of the city, crying, These that have turned the world upside down are come hither also"* (Acts 17:6). We can experience turning our world upside down. We must strive to build a multiple eldership church while discerning the differing callings. We must allow for all callings to minister and take their place. We must promote the ministry of the body. Should we have a mature understanding of the forgoing subjects, we will stumble and fail; if we do not have a deeper, underlying, "foundational truth," we must have humility.

Key Truth, the Soil of Humility

Without planting our church garden in the soil of humility, we will never achieve what our Lord and Savior intends and desires to become a reality. Without humility, we will fail. Humility is the missing oil that makes all of the other fivefold knowledge truths flow together. Humility and servanthood are the missing ingredients that bond the other aspects of knowledge and discernment. When building a house, you have numerous components: wood, concrete, doors, electrical, and so on. It takes knowledge to put these components together. Likewise, when we have a good understanding of callings, eldership, finances, doctrine, and other needful subjects, we have half of the needed truths. The soil of servantheartedness must be in place; lacking humility is the greatest enemy to real church building, as it involves the enemy: "in-a-me," the god of self and image. Holy humility, character, and heartfelt servanthood will determine what our building results will be.

Fivefold church building begins with our humility, achieved by our dethroning of self. Humility crushes our god of self-image. This involves looking to and kneeling before Christ. We desire His image and wishes, as He gives a holy impartation to us, and to others, as well. Make room. Seek for and allow Christ to also use the other callings and elders.

Servanthood to Christ involves more than what I personally do. This involves our acceptance of Christ's Lordship and the Holy Spirit's work through others. Christ calls and appoints. The Holy Spirit imparts gifts, strengths and knowledge to us and other elders as well. We see this truth presented by Apostle Paul: "*Take heed therefore unto yourselves, and to all the flock, over the which the Holy Ghost hath made you overseers, to feed the church of God, which he hath purchased with his own blood*" (Acts 20:28). All of the elders were to minister with a mutual accountability, while overseeing and, also feeding the flock. Denying the work of the

Holy Spirit in fellow elders and believers due to only seeing our own ministry importance is still a sin of self-sufficiency and pride.

Our flesh tends to only focus on what we do and what God does through us. We must seek for the releasing of the Holy Ghost given burdens that He gives to others. Let us not limit others by our lack, by our not discerning their impartations given by the Holy Spirit. We must guide, accept and assist others in their vision. A onefold ministry is as Christ was in His ministry before He lead and matured His following. He changed His focus. He prepared the army to reach the multitudes. May we release all of the elders and saints in their ministry.

Serving Christ in humility and allowing the Holy Spirit to work in building His church will be shown through our actions. Humility will cause eldership to seek for and applaud the ministry of fellow eldership. Humility will also cause us to look for and promote the ministry of the believer. When we blindly do not promote the ministry of the body, we are wrong. If we disregard this truth, we are still planting in the wrong soil of tradition (Eph. 4:12).

Building a fivefold church requires **humility**. John the Baptist was named the greatest of all prophets. His matured conclusion was, *"He must increase, but I must decrease"* (John 3:30). Allow Christ to rise and minister to the body, by the body. The esteeming of others with servant-heartedness is much needed in building.

Elders?

The proof of error is when we have ordained people we name elders and we do not release them to minister. They are also given to "feed" the body, just as we are. Lacking humility by having a onefold ministry is the greatest problem that limits church building. Without the humility of esteeming fellow elders, we will only forge our supposedly spiritual mini-god status, our kingdom versus His Kingdom. We thereby damage Christ's Lordship by disallowing His giving. As Paul taught, *"Let nothing be done through strife or vainglory; but in lowliness of mind let each esteem other better than themselves. Look not every man on his own things, but every man also on the things of others. Let this mind be in you, which was also in Christ Jesus"* (Phil. 2:3–5).

Our Savior humbly demonstrated servanthood when he washed the feet of the apostle servants he was raising up. Likewise, the learned Apostle Paul, in wisdom, wrote:

> *"Who, being in the form of God, thought it not robbery to be equal with God: But made himself of no reputation, and took upon him the form of a servant, and was made in the likeness of men: And being found in fashion as a man, he humbled himself, and became obedient unto death, even the death of the cross. Wherefore God also hath highly exalted him, and given him a name which is above every name".* (Phil. 2:6–9).

Greatness should not be measured by our names or numbers. We must measure by the effects of our ministries, by the mature fruit of those we are bonded to. Humble, Christ-dedicated people are Christ-focused. We covet walking with the Holy Spirit. We do not focus on self-image. The church may love and respect us, but we must worship our Lord.

Esteeming Humility

May we be patient and gentle with all as we see the Holy Spirit's work in the body of believers. The "little others" we minister to may be like a disregarded little shepherd boy. However, God may be preparing a King (1 Sam. 16:11). Never underestimate the power of the Holy Spirit as He works in others. By esteeming what the Lord does by others and through others, we will be stifling that divisionary spirit of competition. Do not measure fellow ministry by what we project. You may provide pepper, while due to a differing burden, calling, vision, or maturity, they may provide salt. Allow toddler steps in the growing process of all. This applies to our fellow elders and ministering believers: *"And we beseech you, brethren, to know them which labor among you, and are over you in the Lord, and admonish you; And to esteem them very highly in love for their work's sake. And be at peace among yourselves"* (1 Thess. 5:12–13). We expect the flock to esteem the elders; we will see greater results in this when visible esteeming is demonstrated by elders for elders and fellow believers.

By edifying, receiving, and encouraging our fellow Christ-appointed ministry, the reality of building fivefold churches will succeed. We must recognize the truth of their being an equally called and Christ-appointed ministry! The Lord desires an army led by five callings.

When we do not esteem and receive the ministry of others, including ministry by the body, we thereby limit the Holy Spirit. Our building focus must be to see the growth and maximization of the entire body. This demands the realignment of focus. In ministry, we fight to be accepted; to be given a platform; to be released in expressing our holy burden and vision. May we "equally" desire this for others within our church body.

When a car's wheels are out of alignment, it will affect the steering ease and tire wear. A onefold ministry of self-focus will likewise affect our steering direction in the church. This will result in discontent, disunity, and unholy, premature wear. Not desiring and welcoming the Fruit of the Holy Spirit's work within our fellow servants is evidence of our lack in our true Christ worship. We must desire a holy Christ-directed army, with all ministering.

To achieve this, we must turn to our God-provided teaching manual. Gleaning manna—the gathering of holy food—requires our in-depth study. Manna consisted of small particles, and it was sweet; it took daily patience and time to gather it. Likewise, knowledge and living by every Word that proceeds from the mouth of God comes by gathering a little at a time: "*Whom shall he teach knowledge? and whom shall he make to understand doctrine? Them that are weaned from the milk, and drawn from the breasts. For precept must be upon precept, precept upon precept; line upon line, line upon line; here a little, and there a little*" (Isa. 28:9–10). When we give what is given to us, more will be given to us (Matt. 13:12).

Unity Is a Must

It grieves my spirit, but I am convinced that it greatly grieves our Lord much more, when supposedly mature ministries and saints will not strive towards unity and esteeming other. To achieve this requires the humility to communicate to dispel differences. This requires maturity. This requires patience and gentleness with genuine loving care.

Without unity we diminish fivefold church building. Recently, I questioned an overseas senior ministry member I was involved with about his conduct and beliefs in certain sinful dealings. I quoted the scriptures involved. He completely avoided the scriptural aspects and responded with an immature personal attack and critique instead. This is common. This behavior will not allow for the building of a fivefold ministry church. Until this changes, I cannot, and will not, be part of building with such. We must have mutual accountability.

CHAPTER TEN:
Fivefold Portrayal: Follow This

Fivefold building: The required demonstration of mature humility . *"Paul and Timotheus, the servants of Jesus Christ, to all the saints in Christ Jesus which are at Philippi, with the bishops and deacons"* (Phil. 1:1). The truth contained in this text must be thoroughly gleaned and lived out. These scriptures contain what has been ignored and read over for many centuries. This portrays the New Testament church in action with a scriptural government. Here we see esteeming with unity. By not thoroughly seeking the value and contents, of this scriptural presentation given to us, we limit fivefold church building.

DANGER: beware of image consciousness. What we see here is so different from what I observe in ministry when I'm traveling. So many people in ministries have an excessive obsession with self-image. Yes, the Lord has called you to the ministry, but avoid a smug pride due to this. We are honored to be His servants, and we prostrate ourselves before His throne while refusing a focus on self-image. We lift up Christ Jesus while desiring His image to be honored above all things, including us. All personal image enhancing limits His image. May we observe the opening statement and honoring of fellow ministry, by the following:

First: This letter was to be distributed to numerous churches, as well as to us. Paul starts this letter with *"Paul and Timotheus."* Herein lies a Christ Lordship truth with humility lived out. Unless we gain this truth, we will always have the ministry of "I," my board, my elders, and so on.

Paul, as a senior "dad apostle," did not write this letter as "I, Paul," as he could have. It is easy to miss the point, here: the point being humble heartedness. Paul had a servant attitude as he acknowledged their growth by esteeming all of his Timothies. Paul honored and visually upheld Timothy before all. This is so needed among elders.

Paul recognized Christ's appointed servants and the result of the Holy Spirit's work in and by them. Paul's love is demonstrated by his honoring the work of Christ in Timothy. This esteeming is often missed. Let us study this by reading five scriptural points of textual truth:

a) Initially, Paul discerned a young man being called of God:

> *"Then came he to Derbe and Lystra: and, behold, a certain disciple was there, named Timotheus, the son of a certain woman, which was a Jewess, and believed; but his father was a Greek: Which was well reported of by the brethren that were at Lystra and Iconium. Him would Paul have to go forth with him; and took and circumcised him because of the Jews which were in those quarters: for they knew all that his father was a Greek".* (Acts 16:1–3)

Timothy proved his servant heart by accepting this circumcision rite as a young man. His relationship to Paul grew and was acknowledged. This voluntary act was to not cause offence. By not doing this, he could have limited the gospel reaching the Jews. I once ate barbequed dog not to limit the gospel to tribal people in the Philippines, a delicacy to them.

b) Later, we see Paul embracing this young man he mentored as a son: *"Unto Timothy, my own son in the faith"* (1 Tim. 1:2). This was said with a loving father's heart (I recommend reading "Not Many Fathers", by Apostle Pete Beck, Jr. [see "Recommended Sources"]). We see a true son in Timothy; he was teachable. He received with respectful ears. Eventually, Paul presents Timothy as an equal in calling and ministry. Not a perpetual top down structure.

c) Paul brought wise counsel to Timothy with holy received insight. He advised Timothy of what to do, rather than encouraging his young head to focus on and idolize his future apostle calling. Nowhere in the scriptures does Paul coach Timothy in regards to how he should carry himself, how he should fit the visible mold of an apostle; Paul only directed him in ministry conduct: *"But watch thou in all things, endure afflictions, do the work of an evangelist, make full proof of thy ministry"* (2 Tim. 4:5). A focus on ministry growth, wisdom, and practical experience is more important than trying to be the future visible calling; this is a common problem based on pride and ego.

d) Apostle Paul demonstrated an example of trust in Timothy, honoring his growing ministry strengths: *"But I trust in the Lord Jesus to send Timotheus shortly unto you, that I also may be of good comfort, when I know your state. For I have no man likeminded, who will naturally care for your state"* (Phil. 2.19–20). This care resulted from Holy-Spirit heart work, the result of seeing the value of the church, along with humbly receiving Paul's mentoring.

e) Paul's relationship expressions grew. With humility, he accepted and upheld his fellow growing ministry members. In time, Paul changed his expression of Timothy from *"my son"* to *"man of God"*: *"But thou, O man of God, flee these things"* (1 Tim. 6:11). Paul humbly upheld, encouraged, and honored this spiritual son. This scripture contains two truths: Timothy was now a "man," signifying ministry maturity. Paul also acknowledged that Timothy belonged to God and not to him, a mistaken posture senior ministries tend to take.

f) The mature Apostle Paul could well have written, "Paul to the church." Instead, Paul commonly wrote, *"Paul, and Silvanus, and Timotheus, unto the church of the Thessalonians"* (1 Thess. 1:1). By holy example, this building attitude demonstrates what we should do. Paul's upholding of honor is observed with his use of "we," "us," and "our" as we read: *"Nor of men sought we glory, neither of you, nor yet of others, when we might have been burdensome, as the apostles of Christ"* (1 Thess. 2:6). This spoke to demeanor and financial dealings. This humble upholding of our fellow ministry, apostles, and elders as equally Christ-appointed is needful and KEY to building the genuine fivefold church.

Second: Paul and Timothy presented themselves as *"the servants of Jesus Christ."* In other letters, Paul introduced himself as *"Paul, a servant of Jesus Christ, a called apostle"* (Rom. 1:1). The point is that Paul had the ministry mindset of being a servant of Christ; this was a priority in to his ministry calling. When we ignore this fact, we have a wrong-hearted demeanor that brings destruction to a servant-minded church. When we present ourselves to others, are we a servant of Christ with humility, or do we assert a "look at me, my achievements, person, and calling?" I personally get convicted by my own writings while presenting this truth.

Christ's second-to-last lesson, just prior to the cross, was with a towel and basin, as He washed the disciple's feet. This humble servant attitude must be demonstrated with maturity, otherwise we will maintain a onefold ministry by building a monument to one's self. This will not exemplify unity, but rather it will destroy unity among the elders; a functioning multiple eldership will be stifled by the pride of *"my* calling."

Third: Paul and Timothy begin the letter by addressing the believer assembly: "the church." This greeting honors the entire church, rather than just offering a prioritized greeting to the fivefold ministry callings and government, whom he addressed afterwards: *"to all the saints in Christ Jesus who are at Philippi."* They honored the church with the term "saints," rather than just "believers." This acknowledged their blood-washed redeemed value, as well as the work of Christ, their being His future bride.

Nowadays, most letters are directed to the pastor, or to other callings. The honoring of *"the saints"* is a huge and much-needed change when building a functional fivefold church. We are limited in our demeanor towards the "saints." With a wrong expectation, we are guilty of sowing a wrong and limiting value that the "saints" now have of themselves. We must mature them to ministry with a higher expectation of them. To have a Biblical fivefold church, we must have a different mindset within all ministry. Then we must teach this mindset to the believers (this insight to be expanded upon).

Fourth: While honoring the saints and family of God, we must honor all men and women, besides elders and deacons, who are full of wisdom and the Holy Spirit. Paul did not disregard ministry government, or their authority and responsibility as he said, *"with the overseers"*; this term ("overseers") includes all the elders, regardless of their callings (Acts 20:17, 28). Together, the elders shared the responsibility of feeding and overseeing the flock. This overseer and feeding responsibility of the plural eldership is a MUST for building a genuine New-Testament-patterned fivefold church. When named elders never present Sunday messages, sin lies at the door.

A holy question is this: do all the elders feed and oversee the people of your church? If not, then why not? The plural eldership, working in unity; both honored and released fellow elders into functional ministry. They did not just give titles; this is a common deficiency that needs correction. We must get beyond just a position or title. This means that all elders are involved in Word-feeding ministry. If not, we did not raise them up properly, or we ordained the wrong elders (1 Tim. 3:2; Acts 20:28). All elders are to minister, teach, and be released into a functional ministry. Have them lead classes teaching foundational doctrine, or have them conduct flock home ministry visitation and exercise their personal ministry focus.

Note: Ministry, flock interaction, and fellowship was different from our Sunday morning church relationships. They experienced personal interaction, *"And they continued steadfastly in the apostles' doctrine and fellowship"* (Act 2:42). This *"apostles' fellowship"* speaks of spending time, discussing with the apostles as family. Not a separation of clergy and laity.

If this is not what we are aiming for, we will greatly limit the church building. We must see and act out the need for the plural ministry and the feeding of the flock by fellow elders. The Ephesian elders were exhorted by Paul: *"Therefore take heed to yourselves, and to all the flock in which the Holy Spirit has made you overseers, to feed the church of God which He has purchased with His own blood"* (Acts 20:28). All of the elders were involved in ministry. All entered into the team ministry of others.

When the apostles heard of the evangelist Philip's ministry fruit in Samaria, they instantly responded and added their ministry strengths

(Acts 8:12–14). Fivefold team work. There is so much loss to the Kingdom when the five callings do not seek out the strengths of others. By ignoring this, we greatly limit the harvest.

Fifth: Deacons are a scripturally needed ministry. The apostles' reference to the deacon ministry is a reality that rarely exists now. The scriptural *term "deacons"* does not fit with most churches. Deacons looked after people—the believer's practical needs—while teaching spiritual maturities. They are a normal part of a mature fivefold church. The deacon ministry did not simply distribute food or money; they also taught the holy wisdom and practical responsibility needed to lead a godly life. In ministry, they exemplified godly wisdom, knowing that those who did not work would not eat. They discerned life realities and they pointed to family responsibilities, a prayerful godliness with diligence (1 Tim. 5:6–16).

Today, this ministry is handcuffed before it starts. Usually, those appointed may be named as such, but they are limited in their functions. Due to programs and ministry salaries, the storehouse tithes and offerings are usually depleted, so that no funds are available. The daily administration to widows and the needy is mostly ignored (Acts 6:1). Deacon ministry must be discussed and faced in order to become a New Testament church. Political correctness will not achieve a genuine fivefold church. Pray, seek, and fight to make this a reality. Address this issue by teaching deacons what to teach, and support the effort to have a genuine, Bible-presented deacon ministry in the churches (1 Tim. 3:13).

The deacon ministry was a viable part of the outpouring and anointing in the Book of Acts. They contributed to the tremendous church growth after the initial deacons were ordained. They released the apostles and elders for their Word ministry and prayer (Acts 6:2).

The deacons' teachings of holy wisdom (the godly principles of life), along with the righteous conduct being applied in practical matters, were part of the first-church explosion and revival: "*And the multitude of those who believed were of one heart and one soul. And not one said that any of the things which he possessed was his own. But they had all things common*" (Acts 4:32). It will take some holy teaching with wisdom and anointing for this renewal to take place. Deacon ministry is a scriptural must. This love and care is part of the gospel being lived out. This brought birth to a genuine fivefold church: "*And the Word of God was increasing. And the number of the disciples in Jerusalem was multiplying exceedingly; even a great crowd of the priests obeyed the faith*" (Acts 6:7). I have not seen this reality properly acted out, including in the churches I carry shared responsibility for. However, with eyes of faith, and by God's Word, I believe in this. Lord, may it be! May we affect the masses and our world! Amen!

CHAPTER ELEVEN:
A Real New Testament Church

Look at a real fivefold church: With a deep yearning in my heart, I long to see what we find in Acts, chapter fifteen. This must become our normal reality. Herein we see the corner stone of truth in regards to what we should be and what we should experience. If we do not desire this reality, expect frustration and an eventual drifting to an apostate church (as so many have). To gain from the truths presented in this chapter, we must deal with the entirety of the chapter (Acts 15:1-36).

Doctrine

This unique chapter begins with a doctrinal question about circumcision: *"And certain ones who came down from Judea taught the brothers, saying, Unless you are circumcised according to the custom of Moses, you cannot be saved"* (Acts 15:1). The question was not without reason. The Word of the Lord to Israel was: *"And the uncircumcised male child whose flesh of his foreskin is not circumcised, that soul shall be cut off from his people; he has broken My covenant"* (Gen. 17:14). Debate arose due to these sincere believers wanting to be right with God in doctrinal matters. Today, many do not care and will avoid discussion. An immature, politically correct people will not seek or take a stand for truth. Our doctrines must be pure and held in unity (1 Cor. 1:10). By mature discussion, we must resolve doctrinal disagreements. We must seek out apostles who will be discerned by their focus on this.

Action and Wisdom

This continues with, *"Therefore dissension and not a little disputation occurring by Paul and Barnabas, they appointed Paul and Barnabas and certain others of them to go up to Jerusalem to the apostles and elders about this question"* (Acts 15:2). They determined to not fail in truth. They acknowledged the seniority maturity of the Jerusalem apostles over the Antioch ministry they were sent out from. They acted in humility. They did not say, "We are apostles. We have the authority and all answers." They sought out fellow apostles, elders, and the church.

Financial Insight

Observe a normal financial practice: *"And indeed being set forward by the church"* (Acts 15:3). Antioch supplied the travel needs for this ministry's journey; Apostle John also taught this financial right (3 John 1:6). Conversely, while staying for a length of time among the believers, the traveling ministry undertook some form of vocation so they would not be burdensome to the churches. Paul thoroughly addressed this while speaking to the Ephesian elders (Acts 20:34).

This was living the example of his teachings, of loving servanthood versus his right. One cannot find different scriptures: *"they which wait at the altar are partakers with the altar? Even so hath the Lord ordained that they which preach the gospel should live of the gospel.* **But** *I have used none of these things: neither have I written these things, that it should be so done unto me"* (1 Cor. 9:13–15). Most stop at verse fourteen when teaching these scriptures.

Being Received

a) *"And arriving in Jerusalem, they were received by the church, and by the apostles and elders"* (Acts 15:4). How is this reception of ministry when we compare to today?

b) They were *"received by the church."* This statement honors the importance and expectation of this assembly when dealing with the believers' church body. A fivefold church will restore this truth with holy insight; they will destroy the unscriptural "laity" word.

c) Here we see esteeming *"by the apostles."* This marks the humble acknowledgment of the correct church ministry authority. It demonstrates the ignored and commonly denied truth of 1 Corinthians, 12:28: *"And God set some in the church, firstly, apostles; secondly, prophets; thirdly, teachers."* It honored the apostle-led, Christ-desired ministry; it was not just being received by the "pastor" (we love and honor pastors).

d) A multiple ministry (*"and elders"*) were acknowledged. They esteemed the entire ordained, and Christ-appointed ministry—not just the apostles (1 Pet. 5:1). This eldership included some of the other four callings, as later demonstrated in this chapter (Acts 15:32).

Normal Problems

We always have the apostate church, which demands a blind upholding of wrong doctrine. They will argue and deny New Testament revelation truth. It seems that there are many who will not listen to the fact that *"all scriptures are profitable for doctrine"* (2 Tim. 3:16). Today, this applies to infant baptism, the baptism of the Holy Spirit, "once saved, always saved" teachings, unconditional love untruth, and much more. Try to reason with them?

Bad doctrines commonly apply, whether they are apostate denominations, evangelicals, or "full gospel" churches that deny fivefold church revelation truths. Doctrinal questioning example, *"But some of those from the sect of the Pharisees, having believed, rose up, saying, It was necessary to circumcise them and to command them to keep the Law of Moses"* (Acts 15:5). We are Christ's ministry and reformers. We destroy sectarian views. In reading about how church doctrine was dealt with, we see the correct authority and the functional responsibility order: *"And the apostles and elders were assembled to see about this matter"* (Acts 15:22). They reasoned this out by using all scriptures (7-21) *"with the whole church."*

The Conclusion Reached

We read, *"Then it pleased the apostles and elders, with the whole church."* Note that we do not just read *"it pleased the apostles and elders"* (Acts

15:22). This scripture demonstrates what must change. We see the proper recognition, discernment, and honoring of the apostle-led leadership.

Consider the inclusion of "it pleased the *whole church.*" This insight begs major change in our thinking and practices. This statement of *"with the whole church"* demonstrates how all were present and welcomed. All of them were expected to be present in this doctrinal reasoning. Everyone could speak to the issue, as it states it pleased *"the whole church."* May this become true today.

The *"whole church"* approved the conclusion and sending of the letter. Make changes to the clergy and laity wall. Expect a greater inclusion and maturity of the saints and their ministry! This must be real in our churches! They decided *"to send chosen men from them to Antioch with Paul and Barnabas; Judas, whose last name was Barsabas; and Silus, chief men among the brothers. And they wrote these things by their hand: The apostles and elders **and brothers** send greeting to <u>the brothers</u>, from the nations in Antioch and Syria and Cilicia"* (Acts 5:22–24). *We have a wrong understanding of how we deal with "the church,"* the believer assembly. We exclude *"brothers"* from such matters. These apostles did not. We must change our views, our treatment, and our expectations of the believer body; this will demonstrate what our Lord desires to have.

We, the eldership ministry, are not intended to be mannequins in God's showcase. We are to be shepherding servants who are called to lift up the body, with expectations of how they are to minister. I often say that "if I am not a brother to you, then forget the apostle title." We have limited the believer's voice, ministry, and growth. The early fivefold church used wisdom and ministered godly inclusion of "the church": *"It seemed good to us, being assembled with one accord* [the apostles, elders, and church]*, to send chosen men to you with our beloved Barnabas and Paul, men who have given up their lives for the name of our Lord Jesus Christ. Therefore we have sent Judas and Silas, who will also announce to you the same things by word"* (Acts 15:25–27).

The Holy Ghost

The Holy Spirit is a key factor when meeting and discussion leading to a decision. We must learn to listen for direction. When we get a check in our spirit, stop and seek out why this is. The entire church and eldership weighed the question of the necessity to circumcise new believers. They prayerfully—with unity, and being in one accord—waited on the Holy Spirit as they debated. As Nehemiah, they sought heaven while discussing with the king. They listened as they debated: *"And the king said to me, For what do you ask? So I prayed to the God of Heaven, and I said to the king"* (Neh. 2:4–5). Listening for heaven's voice is key when dealing with others. Therefore, all present could say: *"For it seemed good to the Holy Spirit and to us to lay on you no greater burden than these necessary things: that you abstain from meats offered to idols, and from blood, and from things strangled, and from fornication; from which, if you keep yourselves, you shall do well. Be prospered"* (Acts 15:28–29).

Ministry humility with holy submission: *"Then indeed they being let go, they came to Antioch. And gathering the multitude, they delivered the letter"* (Acts 15:30). What a statement! Note: unlike today, Antioch and Jerusalem honored *"the multitude,"* while we dishonor the "multitude" our church believer body.

The submissive humility of *"being let go,"* as demonstrated by mature prophets, is rare today and refreshing. May this be; they acted in unity with the leadership and body. A Jezebel spirit says, "me and God! I will go and do only what God tells me." These prophets, considered the entire church body. With hearts of humility and love, they wanted all to be comfortable with their actions.

The Jezebel spirit (which is to be avoided) involves the refusal of some to work with patient unity, thereby disregarding God-given authority. This does not mean simply having a disagreement about a decision or direction; that is allowed, and it may be good. Not discussing, however, is a lack of submitting one to another. This is evidenced by the manipulation, anger, and tearing of unity where very little patience to reason is shown. This will be demonstrated in how some leave a church fellowship, by expressing anger with a tearing of any and all there. This anger will especially be focused towards the leadership who refused to be bulldozed. Godly people prove their godliness by how they leave.

Natural Ministry

Ministry with Holy Ghost wiring will hit an "on" switch when under God: *"And Judas and Silas, also being prophets themselves, exhorted the brothers with many words and confirmed them"* (Acts 15:32). These prophets, who were named elders in verse four, were quickened by Holy-Spirit unction. They naturally did what prophets do: they *"confirmed them."* Prophetic affirmation strengthened these church believers, establishing them in their individual walk and direction before God.

This shows us what is lacking today, both in the submission of ministry and the recognition of the fivefold church governmental authority. *"And remaining for a time, they were let go in peace from the brothers to the apostles"* (Acts 15:33). Note: this does not say they returned to the City of Jerusalem, or the Jerusalem church, but *"to the apostles."*

This honoring of scriptural authority as unto Christ is strongly needed, but disregarded. When the church begins to work in unity, following a scriptural order of the called holy ministry as it is set out, we will have some of what "fivefold ministry churches" portray. There was a respectful "mutual accountability." They respectfully allowed the heart burden of the fellow ministries to be released as the Holy Spirit led; *"But it pleased Silas to remain there"* (Acts 15:34). This Bible-portrayed body ministry is devoid of a leadership that acts with a spirit of control. We must revise our thoughts and gain a scriptural expectation of the believer body in ministry. The church is not a corporation with a commanding officer ruling management, along with supervisors and managers; the church is a love-based body that respectfully submits to all parts while also acknowledging authority of different ministry callings, and roles (such as "helps and governments") as well as the different spiritual gifts.

In scripture, we also see the interweaving and function of the multiple ministry order: *"Also Paul and Barnabas continued in Antioch, teaching and preaching the gospel, the Word of the Lord, with many others also"* (Acts 15:35). Oh Lord, may this become a church reality. They humbly made room for each other.

Then we see the genuine burden of the apostle calling: *"And some days afterward, Paul said to Barnabas, Let us go again and visit our brothers in every city where we have announced the Word of the Lord, to see how they are holding to it"* (Acts 15:36). The care of all the churches is fundamental to any mature apostle. They, as a mother, will never forget their church children.

Painful Truth

Recently, while in Canada, I met a gifted and anointed couple. He is a prophet who has a long ministry history of traveling to numerous countries. She has a gifted voice and has led worship in major events. They just got married and are expecting a child while in their late thirties. Now they will be more focused in settling down with a home base, other than future traveling in ministry. Both of them come from a background of ministry. How will they fit into a local full gospel church? His calling makes him equal to or greater in authority than a pastor.

How will they be received in ministry? Also, the question is: has this anointed, gift ministry prophet grown to mature as an elder, with a responsibility for a local flock and an elder's heart? Will they be forced to start their own work, or will they be embraced and received as a fellow elder? This is a two-sided problem. The established churches may deem the couple to be an independent ministry, while the independent spirit of these churches limits their reaching out to them.

This I know: there is no recognized and mature apostle in their community or lives. If there was, and the apostle was received by all, this would bring positive change to these circumstances, the church and ministry direction, and the stability and joy of all. There are many more solo ministries who are disconnected. In this location, two gifted ministries just held a series of meetings with no local church attachments or being receiving. Lord! Raise up mature apostles. May they be discerned and received. May order come to the churches!

CHAPTER TWELVE:
The Building Mindset of a Reformer

Change needed: The genuine "fivefold church" will only be built by those who see this as a needed scriptural truth. Seeing the evidence by the fact that, in many ways, the church and ministry of today are not comparable to what the scriptures portray. At a minimum, the building of a fivefold church involves:

a) A separate experiential baptism of the Spirit, attended with tongues and prophecy.

b) Gifts of the Spirit being normal to those baptized in the Spirit.

c) Recognition of the five differing Christ-appointed ministry callings.

d) A multiple ministering eldership with mutual accountability.

e) A very different and scriptural outlook of the believer's ministry.

f) An apostle-led governmental structure. This scriptural, Christ-given and desired church government is denied by all denominations and most independent churches! Building a genuine fivefold church will require departure from what mostly exists. This will require an open-minded study of Holy Scripture in order to determine the truths of this claim. While watching the news about current political matters and a grueling battle for the presidential nominee, a commentator said, "One has to want it badly to stay in the race." This truth applies; reformers who want to see a scriptural New Testament church must want it badly!

Zealous Drive

Regarding Christ Jesus, salvation, and His eternal government, Isaiah said that *"the zeal of the Lord shall perform it"* (Isa. 9:7). This zeal took Christ past the cross: *"Looking unto Jesus the author and finisher of our faith; who for the joy that was set before him endured the cross, despising the shame, and is set down at the right hand of the throne of God"* (Heb. 12:2).

Likewise, we, as reformers, must also be cloaked with holy zeal. Holy zeal starts with seeing, believing, and desiring what we read in the scriptures. Believing and seeing with holy hunger will produce holy vision! In order to see what our Lord gave and what He wants the church to be and have, we must see the scriptural church examples that were made possible by His Word! Wage zealous warfare for truth; at the end, we will also find our rest, both now and at the Father's throne.

With a strong desire, I want to do my part of the mission, of building churches that are comparable to what the New Testament portrays. Reformer warriors of faith will scripturally see the need for—and seek to achieve—what our Lord of the church desires. Miracles, healing, and revelation gifts are for today. We must work for a unified, knowledgeable church, where all are involved when a Paul and Barnabas visit to clarify doctrinal matters—a church where all are expected to understand and be involved in discerning doctrinal truth.

We must shun what personal ambition will draw our ministry to. Will we lay down our lives and reputations and do whatever it takes for Christ and His church? We must seek how we can establish what should be. Change involves implementing the following:

a) A knowledge of the Word in regards to Christ-given ministry callings, as well as the ability to discern these callings.

b) Having a scriptural knowledge of Christ's desired government, His church with a holy desire to establish this now. We MUST HAVE SPIRITUAL HUNGER!

c) A strong surrendering to Christ while forsaking selfish ambition (or our focus on meeting people's expectations). We are the Lord's servants and desire what He desires.

d) Correct Bible doctrinal beliefs. May all be desirous of patiently resolving differences.

e) Servanthood with humility, forsaking the god of "I" by kneeling to Christ's Lordship.

f) Revising our common understanding of the ministry of the believer body.

g) Seeking humility, a strong worship of God, Christ, and His Lordship. This focus will steadily put to death the fear of man. This will enthrone Christ by revealing Bible truth.

Holy Vision, Seeing the Reality

For those who see the need of a rightful scriptural fivefold church, **these last three listed requirements are more relevant. They** deal with the god of self. Applying these truths will enhance and result in the real building of a genuine fivefold church.

We must digest and strongly apply truths imparted by Isaiah. By holy anointing direction, He directs us: "*Go through, go through the gates; prepare ye the way of the people; cast up, cast up the highway; gather out the stones; lift up a standard for the people*" (Isa. 62:10).

There are a number of things to observe as we read this scripture. Isaiah projects a progressive truth revelation, beginning with Isaiah, chapter six. We must see the holy glory of God and our personal unclean lips that must be touched by the coal from the altar. Unsanctified flesh will not achieve God's ministry and building. Mouthed evil thoughts are from the heart (Matt. 15:18).

This continues with ministry revelation. The Spirit of the Lord is upon us with divine purpose (Isa. 61:1). This continues with instructions to enable and enhance the gospel going to the ends of the earth (Isa 62:10). These revelation truths must to be applied in fivefold church building.

a) "*Go through, go through the gates.*" We must enter, then receive from Him in order to do His bidding. These twelve temple entrance gates, are what use for man to meet with God. Twelve is the number of God's government on earth (twelve tribes of Israel, twelve apostles, and twenty-four elders in heaven (2 x 12), the eternal government (Gen.

41:32; Rev. 4:10). Christ's government with His Fivefold Lordship (five, the number for grace; fifty, the year of Jubilee, Pentecost). This involves the unified truths of five and twelve, God's grace and government. When we establish His government, many seekers will enter His presence through His restored government, as we mend the government gates.

b) We need to rebuild the burned gates. Nehemiah dealt with the remains of the burned temple's skeleton. God's judgment allowed the destroying of these gates, due to the people's spiritual death. Nehemiah rebuilt the gates. Rebuilding fivefold ministry churches is like rebuilding the temple gates through Christ's desired government. Many believers will enter when the gates are renewed. Israel's first general assembly during the temple restoration was to read the scriptures at the "water gate"; the only gate which was not destroyed was the water gate, as the Word of God has never been destroyed (Eph. 5:25–26; Neh. 3:26, 8:1).

c) Our mandate is: "*prepare ye the way of the people; cast up, cast up the highway; gather out the stones.*" Build a road that people can easily traverse. This is a heavenly assignment given to us, His ministry priesthood. This message is spoken to the entire believing church—not just the ministry elders or the five-gift callings! Teach wisdom and non-negotiable Bible truths in ministry.

d) To build a highway through wilderness terrain is not easy. However, when this highway is complete, it will greatly enhance the travel of those seeking salvation and their relationship with a Holy God. We must remove the stones and impediments of wrong doctrine, wrong spiritual demeanor, financial focus, and loveless pride. These stones impede travel as people trip over them.

e) Our mandate is, "*lift up a standard for the people.*" The standard we must lift up is Bible truth and what the cross portrays. This "*standard for the people*" includes the scriptural church and ministry. We demonstrate the standard by our humility before Christ. We live a life of progressively being drawn into an obedience walk led by the Holy Spirit; this life involves our church's fellowship as we are "*baptized into one body*" (1 Cor. 12:13). It involves our love, as well as our esteeming ministry relationships in the entire body. This includes the eldership, the government of God, and the ministry of the body we oversee.

Christ's Lordship

The Bible and New Testament portray a church that has a Christ-recognized Lordship. We do not have this today; we only claim to have it. We deny Christ's fivefold church ministry government with no scriptural basis for the change from what He gives and sets in His church. Instead, we demonstrate a confusing picture to the unsaved, seeking world. We demonstrate a mosaic picture of the religiously unsaved and the legalists demanding righteousness by keeping laws, as well the extremes of a false humanistic liberty. We must demonstrate Christ's ministry government by a loving leadership proclaiming the gospel of grace with truth.

Praise God! There are genuine believers in many churches who contrast this neglect; they are glimpses of light, showing through the fog. Godly ministry is seeking to bring change by revealing the true church under Christ. We thank God for churches that preach the infallibility of scriptures as well as the believer's personal salvation by being born of the Spirit. People are getting saved regardless of the lack that exists in our church ministries. Thank God for those who teach and minister the baptism of the Holy Spirit and uphold the gifts of the Holy Spirit. However, millions more will be saved when we come under the cloud of God's relational presence and obediently build tents, tabernacles, and churches by Christ's pattern.

The devil masks, twists, destroys, and hides truth in the spiritual battle. He attempted to derail Christ in his wilderness temptations. WHAT makes us think that he is not doing his all to derail us and our church building to limit the gospel? This is the reality of our warfare. Through the truths revealed in God's Word, genuine ministries will expose the false ones. When we are not determined to radically yield to the Word, we fail. The Word sets out God's desire and His will. Ignoring fivefold ministry is saying to the Lord, "Our ways are higher than yours." How can preachers deny the scriptures detailing the given multiple ministry callings and God's established authority order?

Maturity Measuring

A mature fivefold church will be measured by the depth, maturity, and ministry of the believer assembly. The maturity of the saints' ministries will be seen by their fruit—the result of their dedication to Christ. In our holy pattern, we are shown the effect of their ministry: *"These that have turned the world upside down are come hither also"* (Acts 17:6). This was the church and not just elders and called ministry. Arise, and fight for this! We do not have this church today. We must!

It is painful to see the reasons for this. Several years ago, I shared a book I had authored called *Destroyed Foundations* with a local Pentecostal pastor nearing retirement. After reading it, his response was, "Yes, this is truth, but I am near retirement, and those after me will need to bring change." He saw the truths, but was not willing to stand for them. He was not willing to pay the price of his denominational rejection.

OH Lord! May we count and be willing to pay the cost to bring change? Many do not want to rock their comfortable boat, not wanting to offend man. By their inaction, however, they are willing to offend God! Seeking out Word truths and applying them is real worship. God told Jeremiah that wrong must be uprooted, torn down, and destroyed before we plant and sow correction. "Destroy"? Many look for "unity" so that everyone can get along. We also wish for unity, but truth is nonnegotiable, and it is our standard. The Bible says, *"How can two walk together unless they agree?"* (Amos 3:3) Many succumb to just seeking peace with all named "Christians." Yes, the truth is that seeking peace is a godly pursuit. Jesus taught, *"Blessed are the peacemakers: for they shall be called the children of God"* (Matt. 5:9). This is a one-text truth that needs to be balanced with what Christ Jesus also taught:

> *"Think not that I am come to send peace on earth: I came not to send peace, but a sword. For I am come to set a man at variance against his father, and the daughter against her mother, and the daughter in law against her mother in law. And a man's foes shall be they of his own household. He that loves father or mother more than me is not worthy of me"*. (Matt. 10:34–37)

Seek peace, but not at the cost of silencing the truth.

CHAPTER THIRTEEN:
A Ministry of Mature Fivefold Saints

Fivefold ministry involves changing our expectations of the saints. When we receive the scriptures that set out the standard, our entire church view of the believer's ministry will change. The five-gift ministries and elders are given: "*For the perfecting of the saints, for the work of the ministry, for the edifying of the body of Christ*" (Eph. 4:12).

This verse can be read in two ways. First, we can read it as saying that the five ministry callings are to mature the saints, thereby edifying the saints and the body of Christ. Second, we can read it as saying that the five callings are to mature the saints so that they are prepared for their ministry; this results in the ministering of matured saints. They will edify the body and minister to unbelievers, as well.

My belief is that both are correct. When mature, the church body members will minister to the body as Paul taught, where "*every joint supplies*." When the saints edify the body, it means doing more than singing in the choir or helping with kitchen and janitorial duties. Please review the entire passage verse by verse; these are the fivefold scriptural rules of engagement, given by the Lord for all the churches. [Ministries are given]

> "*for the perfecting of the saints, for the work of the ministry, for the edifying of the body of Christ: Till we all come in the unity of the faith, and of the knowledge of the Son of God, unto a perfect man, unto the measure of the stature of the fullness of Christ: That we henceforth be no more children, tossed to and fro, and carried about with every wind of doctrine, by the sleight of men,*

and cunning craftiness, whereby they lie in wait to deceive; But speaking the truth in love, may grow up into him in all things, which is the head, even Christ: From whom the whole body fitly joined together and compacted by that which every joint supplies, according to the effectual working in the measure of every part, makes increase of the body unto the edifying of itself in love" (Eph. 4:12–16).

Denial of this scripture is a denial of Christ, His giving, and His Lordship!

These scriptures contain the Holy Truths of our Christ-given ministry mandate; this is what a fivefold called ministry and the believer body are to attain in a matured church.

Facetious but True: Those Who Deny This Giving Must Have Reached a Conclusion of:

a) The saints are all involved in doing the work of the ministry.
b) The saints are all in unity.
c) The saints are knowledgeable to the measure of Christ.
d) The saints are mature and not children.
e) The saints are doctrinally knowledgeable.
f) The saints all minister edification to the body.
g) The onefold ministry has brought them to maturity.

Consider the following scripture: *"Till we **all** come in the unity of the faith, and of the knowledge of the Son of God, unto a perfect man, unto the measure of the stature of the fullness of Christ" (Eph. 4:13)*. Elders and *"all"* are to be mature. If this is not what we have, or what our church's expectation is, we will fall short of a real fivefold reality. This *"all"* leads to the maturity measure of *"the fullness of Christ."* This involves knowledge and spiritual growth given by the Holy Spirit. All must seek holy presence— a life of hearing, obedience, and ministry on a relational walk with the Holy Spirit. This underscores the need to mature believers beyond the "baby" stage. Begin by teaching foundational doctrines! (Heb. 6:1)

All elders and believers need to change from what currently exists. This is a tall order, but it's scripturally possible, and it's not an unreasonable expectation. Part of the purpose of this change is as follows: *"That we henceforth be no more children, tossed to and fro, and carried about with every wind of doctrine, by the sleight of men, and cunning craftiness, whereby they lie in wait to deceive"* (Eph. 4:14).

The winds of doctrine constantly come from both the cults and inside the church. The Church of Latter Days Saints (Mormons) and the Jehovah's Witnesses (Russelites) all knock on doors with their evangelizing. They train their people two to three nights a week and enforce the ministry of their people. They are a works- and law-focused people. Our ministry efforts should be initiated and discerned as the results of our faith and love for Christ.

The cults are well versed in what they twist; they learn how to pervert what real churches teach by "term-switching" key doctrinal words. "Term-switching" means saying the right words but having a personally different meaning to these words. The cults are well trained in presenting their falsehood to seem as if they agree with real church teachings. They learn to twist their denial of the deity of Christ. They pervert by term-switching to deceive the unknowing. Always ask them, "What do words like **'being born again'** mean to you?" They deny the church doctrine of eternal judgment; ask them what "eternal judgment" means to them. Unless the believer is thoroughly grounded in the foundational doctrines, they will not be able to stand and debate their lies.

A highly credible Christian organization posted that 75 percent of cult adherents are gained from nominal Christian churches that do not ground their people in doctrine. Ministry elders are responsible for maturing the saints; when matured, they will be less vulnerable to *"the sleight of men, and cunning craftiness, whereby they lie in wait to deceive"* (Eph. 4:14). When we mature the saints by teaching the apostle's doctrine, they will be less vulnerable (Heb. 5:11–6:2).

Grow Up

We are to *"grow up into Him in all things"*; this is the ministry mandate that needs to be met. This takes a multiple eldership who will learn and then teach doctrine to the saints.

THIS IS THE NUT; this is the central truth of *"the whole body fitly joined together and compacted by that which every joint supplies"* (Eph. 4:16). All of them are to do more than bless the offering plate, but this will not happen without the maturing of the saints. When a mature eldership ministry is working together, this will be possible. This takes evening study classes. Only matured saints will be enabled to effectively do what follows, *"according to the effectual working in the measure of every part."* Real increase and not just in attendance comes with promoting real body ministry These are Bible-written instructions These should be our expectation. This is what it takes to achieve the result of *"[making] increase of the body unto the edifying of itself in love"* (Eph. 4:16).

Yes, we encourage a loving-family social interaction with our church family. However, maturing them doctrinally protects the believers from wrong doctrine within the church.

A current example is the dangerous lie and untruth of "God's unconditional love.", the belief that regardless of what believers do after getting saved they will be in heaven.   This has damaged many people in my area of North Idaho. It leads to partaking of presumptuous sin. David presumed on God's love when with Bathsheba; he thought he was strong (Ps. 19:13). A family baptized in the Holy Ghost who attends a "full gospel" church that strongly embraces the "once saved, always saved" theology completely swallowed this untruth. Now, a few years later, they believe practicing homosexual people who "believe in Jesus" will also be in heaven. Rather than warning homosexuals of the sin of homosexuality, some, with the intention of expressing "God's love," walked with them in a gay parade with signs of "God loves homosexuals." They are blind to the truth that those who embrace this sinful lifestyle will be judged and in hell (1 Cor. 6:9).

There is nothing we receive from God that does not involve meeting His conditions. Yes, God wholly loves man enough to make Jesus and the cross available, BUT we must read God's promises; they all have attached conditions. To receive from God, we must always choose to meet His conditions. Two out of a hundred examples are *"But as many as received him, to them gave he power to become the sons of God, even to them that believe on his name"* (John 1:12). We are enabled to become *"the sons of God,"* but only if we *"believe on his name"*; this is our choice. Then, also, *"For God so loved the world, that he gave his only begotten Son, that whosoever believes in him should not perish, but have everlasting life"* (John 3:16). God's giving of love to "whosoever" is lost on the unbelieving. They will *"perish."* God's promises always have an "IF" attached for us to meet.

Holy Truth

Mature your people by teaching them to defend their knowledge; this is our elder responsibility. Yes, we are to pray and care for churches and Christians at large. They operate with the revelation they have and believe. However, a truth given by the Holy Spirit that I have learned is that I am not responsible for those who are not accountable to me. Also, we are very much responsible for those who are given to us (John 17:6–8; Matt. 18:23). Do not waste time or resources on those who are not accountable to your ministry. Receiving accolades and tickling ears is not church building! Build teachable and accountable ears; encourage those who follow us in what we are given.

Guard against error. Mature saints and churches will discern and shun an imbalanced prosperity gospel. We believe in our gracious God of blessing, but an imbalanced focus on this is dangerous. The sown seed that grew up but was choked, eliminating holy fruitfulness, is described here: *"The cares of this world, and the deceitfulness of riches and the lusts of other things entering in, choke the word, and it becometh unfruitful"* (Mark 4:19).

Many megachurches focus too much on a message of "me and my blessed life of prosperity"; they become "megachurches" by tickling ears in this way. They never hear Bible messages on sin and the coming judgment, or the loss and hell ahead for the ungodly. They ignore a sacrificial life to reach others with a love and concern for their souls. We must also teach what they usually avoid. Judgment with damnation and a coming hell is part of the real gospel. When these truths are not presented as part of the menu, along with the gospel blessings, people are on shaky ground. Imbalanced believers are not taught to pray without ceasing, or to carry and share in Christ's burden of souls to avoid hell damnation . The focus on a "me" life needs the balance of *"Christ lives in me: and the life which I now live in the flesh I live by the faith of the Son of God, who loved me, and gave himself for me"* (Gal. 2:20).

Some who consider this to be an unjust critique need to listen to some of the popular existing messages from megachurches and broad-gate assembly preachers. You will be hard-pressed to find the word "judgment" mentioned, and never the fear of hell. We do believe the blessings of joy and peace are part of a victorious Christian life. Jesus said He came to give us abundant life when we *"first seek the Kingdom of God"*; then all things will be added to us. However, a real Christ-hearted love will be demonstrated and include what Jesus preached by the real gospel. His love ministry to the lost started with, *"From that time Jesus began to preach, and to say, Repent: for the kingdom of heaven is at hand"* (Matt. 4:17). Repentance and our renewal in Christ is a Godly focus. Sanctification is by the blood but also by our responsibility (1 Thess. 4:3).

Likewise, Paul the Apostle did not just preach our "sugar rights," but also the needed reality of the coming judgment: *"And as he reasoned of righteousness, temperance, and judgment to come, Felix trembled"* (Acts 24:25). Those who avoid these topics are of a wrong focus. Preach these truths, as well. Be courageous. We in ministry defend our flock by this, just as Jesus did!

With the joy of our salvation, we desire His presence. Then we will see life and others through "Christ glasses." We rejoice in His loving care. I warn believers from following those who do not balance messages of blessing with His coming hell and judgment truths. Balanced truth will cause us to seek the saving of mankind and avoid horrible judgment. That is love!

Doctrinal Maturity of the Ministering Saints

Knowledge will strengthen believers to resist from falling away (2 Pet. 1:9–10). Knowledge prepares them with a capability for a life of ministry. All the foundational doctrines speak to our life in Christ. Deeply learning the six foundational doctrines brings focus and vision to the saints. Part of the intent of *"forsake not the assembling of yourselves"* is to maintain clarity of focus. Several scriptures point out what we are to "remember" (2 Thess. 2:5; Jude 1:17). Keeping these truths fresh and clear in the believers' minds will affect the believers' priorities. Maturing believers doctrinally will strengthen their resolve to seek eternal matters. Knowledge will encourage them in their ministry to affect the lives of others with eyes of eternity.

All believing saints are expected to project light and be salt by the knowledge of the gospel of Christ. Political correctness is often rooted in weakness and the immaturity of love and our purpose. Real maturity leads to the love and strength to act: *"Brethren, if a man be overtaken in a fault, ye which are spiritual, restore such a one in the spirit of meekness"* (Gal. 6:1).

It takes real love to confront sin along with a spirit of meekness. It takes real love to hear others out when they differ from you. It takes a mature patience to dialogue with others when we think our understanding is obviously the only truth. The mature will seek to be of one mind. Always apply "all scriptures" when seeking to become of one mind (2 Tim. 3:16). By seeking truth, the saints demonstrate their real love for Christ.

Are the saints matured? Listen to their conversation. Are they *"speaking the truth in love"*? Are they striving to *"grow up into him in all things, which is the head, even Christ"*? The Bible is clear about this topic: *"Then they that feared the LORD spoke often one to another: and the LORD hearkened, and heard it, and a book of remembrance was written before him for them that feared the LORD, and that thought upon his name"* (Mal. 3:16). May we mature the saints by a multiple functioning eldership? Just attending a Sunday morning service will not facilitate this. The first church did. How? They *"continued steadfastly in the apostles' doctrine and fellowship, and in breaking of bread, and in prayers."* Build as they did!

All the elders are to feed the flock. The ministry of the body and the spiritual realm is more than a spectator sport. More than their financial giving, they are to build the body by their ministry. We need servant-heartedness in practical matters. We applaud the ushers, but must realign our expectation of the body ministry—that is, we must align it to as *"it is written*." God's Word teaches a form of church building where "*every part, makes increase of the body unto the edifying of itself in love.*" Be honest. When every part of the ministry does not contribute, we maintain a spectator sport for fans.

Ordination and Real Believer Growth

We must understand this; all believers are an ordained people. As it reads in John,

> "*No longer do I call you servants, for the servant does not know what his master does. But I have called you friends, for all things that I have heard from My Father I have made known to you. You have not chosen Me, but I have chosen you **and ordained you** that you should go and bring forth fruit*". (John 15:15–16)

Do we teach our following about their ordination? Do we teach them that they are called to ministry, and do we teach them to be fruitful?

We must teach every part of the body their scriptural expectation. This is a key truth to "real growth." When leadership creates fellowship gatherings, with an environment for this, great things will happen. God cannot lie. His Word is established in heaven. Honestly face this truth. When so much of the body is not compacted together, and not ministering or receiving by "*which every joint supplies*," we need to seek the Lord for change. To bring change will involve a multiple eldership ministry. One elder cannot do this.

The following text speaks to the heart of this matter: "*the effectual working in the measure of every part.*" That is not a "baby believer's" expectation. This states that all parts are to mature and be involved in body-edification ministry. All of them are to minister faith, knowledge, Bible, and the anointing impartation of the Holy Spirit. Our expectation of the body must be that it "*makes increase of the body unto the edifying of itself in love.*" This, my fellow ministries and believers, is a higher standard than what exists. This is the Bible's standard of Christ in regards to what should be in His church.

This is part of what produced the world's explosion of gospel. This explosion must and will occur again.

Joel's Latter Rain

Joel's early rain is past, and the latter rain is coming. The Word promises two rain events: "*Be glad then, ye children of Zion, and rejoice in the LORD your God: for he has given you the former rain moderately, [moderately] and he will cause to come down for you the rain, the former rain, and the latter rain*" (Joel 2:23). The former rain was Pentecost, and it has already come. Be glad! The sons and daughters prophesied and had visions. Now, rejoice, for the latter rain is coming. We are experiencing the first few drops, but expect the downpour. This will produce the army in a way we have never seen before, In the day of the Lord, the rapture (Joel 2:1–12). The sun will be darkened, and the moon will turn to blood before that great day. The Antichrist shall be revealed before Christ's coming (Joel 2:28–31; 2 Thess. 2:8).

God's promise: "*And it shall come to pass afterward, that I will pour out my spirit upon all flesh; and your sons and your daughters shall prophesy, your old men shall dream dreams, your young men shall see visions: And also upon the servants and upon the handmaids in those days will I pour out my spirit*" (Joel 2:28–29; Zech. 10:1). Most deny "*all flesh.*"

Prepare for this. Expect the ministry of daughters, young men, and old servant men.

Today, our heavenly Father is waiting for the latter-day harvest: "*Be patient therefore, brethren, unto the coming of the Lord. Behold, the husbandman waits for the precious fruit of the earth, and hath long patience for it, until he receives the early and latter rain*" (James 5:7). Apostle John tells the church to be patient. The fruit of the early rain of Pentecost is past. Now, expect what the Father (husbandman) is waiting for: the fruit of the "latter rain."

Corinth Church Gatherings and Ours

We have many church gatherings and worship formats in both denominational and independent churches. Real fivefold churches will and must be guided by commonly ignored scriptures. The reality of how we are to conduct our worship fellowship services is found in 1 Corinthians, chapter 14. This starts with teachings about prophecy and tongues in church services (14:1–25). Then we have our fellowship gathering instructions: "*How is it then, brethren? When you come together, every one of you has a psalm, has a doctrine, has a tongue, has a revelation, has an interpretation. Let all things be done unto edifying*" (1 Cor. 14:26). Where is this happening?

THIS IS NOT commonly happening. This is not our usual expectation. I hunger for this maturity to come forth. I want to be part of services where "*every one of you,*" under the anointing, "*has a psalm, doctrine, tongue, revelation, has an interpretation.*" This may not be what we have right now, but it never will be unless we believe for and desire it to be.

When you look at our circumstances, do not be mentally blocked by your disbelief; instead, look to and believe the scriptures with a holy pursuit of this becoming a reality. This requires change. This involves an environment in our fellowship services that is conducive to making this change possible. This involves planning with purpose—that is, having an environment of Holy-Spirit liberty, with less formality—in order to birth this expectation.

We must also respect the longer expository preaching. Scriptures support this; for example: "*a certain young man named Eutychus, being fallen into a deep sleep: and as Paul was long preaching*" (Acts 20:9). Paul needed more time to release his heart burden for the church—that is, the message he shared at length. This lengthy speaking does not erase the instructions for gathering, where all the church body may—and should—be involved.

Remember: the instantly moving "living creatures" only heard God's voice after letting their wings down (Ezek. 1:25). To hear the Lord, we must stop our busyness and worship.

CHAPTER FOURTEEN:
The Believer's Ministry - a Fivefold Must

Live branches will bear fruit; thus, a believer's ministry and fruitfulness is a must. This proves the branches attached to Christ are still alive. "Alive" means a genuine love for Christ—a hot love, and not a lukewarm love that Christ will spit out on the Day of Judgment (Rev. 3:16). We need a faith that is alive and proven by our works: *"For as the body without the spirit is dead, so faith without works is dead also"* (James 2:26). All right-hearted ministries will stem from our worship of Him—He who loved us enough to endure the cross. This profound love will cause us to love Him by fulfilling His heart's desire. His heart's faithful grace is seen by the continual salvation of souls. We love Him, His people and reach out to win souls, as demonstrated by our ministering to our fellow man.

While we weigh the ministry of the church—both the elders and flock ministry—may we not ignore the relevancy of Christ's Words in John, chapter fifteen. To gain insight, this entire scripture must be reviewed. Here, Jesus Christ deals with the ministry of the church body, by our abiding in Him; as well as the results of failing to do so:

> *"I am the true vine, and my Father is the husbandman. Every branch in me that bears not fruit he takes away: and every branch that bears fruit, he purges it, that it may bring forth more fruit. Now ye are clean through the word which I have spoken unto you. Abide in me, and I in you. As the branch cannot bear fruit of itself, except it abide in the vine; no more can ye, except ye abide in me. I am the vine, ye are the branches: He that abides in me, and I in*

him, the same bring forth much fruit: for without me ye can do nothing. If a man abide not in me, he is cast forth as a branch, and withers; and men gather them, and cast them into the fire, and they are burned. If ye abide in me, and my words abide in you, ye shall ask what ye will, and it shall be done unto you. Herein is my Father glorified, that ye bear much fruit; so shall ye be my disciples. As the Father hath loved me, so have I loved you: continue ye in my love". (John 15:1)

This teaching by Christ is a heavy-duty presentation. Several of Jesus' teachings present this focus. The summarization of this is: our Lord speaks to the need for us to enter into and then maintain a sincere, abiding love and fruitful relationship with God. Not just for a few months, but as a lifelong pursuit. This requires our single-minded perseverance. In regards to the Israelites, who left Egypt, the following is true: "*And all the people answered together, and said, All that the LORD hath spoken we will do*" (Exod. 19:8). Then after this, they murmured, spoke of stoning Moses, and made a golden calf. This is why so few entered the Promised Land. We face a similar potential.

Again, our heavenly Father exhorts all of us to abide in Christ. Do not lose focus. This will be achieved by a fruit-bearing, focused, covenant people. The details are:

1. "*I am the true vine, and my Father is the husbandman.*" Christ speaks of Himself being the vine. The believers are the branches who receive life from Christ, the vine. Our heavenly Father is the gardener. We, the believers, are souls in our Lord's garden. The world is still the wilderness.

2. "*Every branch in me that bears not fruit he takes away.*" This is a terrible truth that many avoid in their theology. All believers should be aware of this truth. Branches connected to Christ can be "*taken away*; this occurs when believers in Christ, the vine, do not produce fruit. Fruit is the evidence of abiding life. Jesus spoke this to believers "*in Him.*" The fruit of the good works of the unsaved will not merit salvation (Eph. 2:8–9).

Note: *"Every branch"* involves the fruit of every believer; all are ministry—not just the fivefold eldership. The focal topic is to bear fruit, as sanctified branches by abiding in Christ. We know faith must be alive; this faith is proven by our works: *"Even so faith, if it hath not works, is dead, being alone. Yea, a man may say, you hast faith, and I have works: show me thy faith without thy works, and I will shew thee my faith by my works"* (James. 2:17–18).

These Bible scriptures and theology is a much-needed study. All believers in Christ need to press in to be fruitful. We can wander into a wrong life's focus; thereby, we can no longer abide in Christ. So many believers simply sit from week to week, looking for a glorious, earthly, self-seeking life as they wait for heaven. The believer flock needs enlightenment. They need to abide daily in order to be a Christ-seeking, life-pursuing people imbued with the presence of the Holy Spirit. Fruitlessness will be due to religiosity while seeking a self-life. Fruitfulness is an automatic result of a Christ-seeking, Holy-Spirit-pursuing life. Meditate on His Word. Pray without ceasing.

Every spring, my maintained apple tree faithfully produces spring flowers, resulting in a crop of apples. Likewise, in a living sacrifice ministry, fruitfulness is a natural result (Rom. 12:1). So many do not maintain or abide! Beware! Non-fruit-bearing branches are *"taken away."* This is why our Savior told Sardis and all churches the following: *"You have a few names even in Sardis who have not defiled their garments. And they will walk with Me in white, for they are worthy"* (Rev. 3:4).

When we see the greatness of God the Father's love—that is, what He gives us through Christ in our redemption—our entire life's focus should change. Our lives should then respond to His love as we seek His heart's desires. We should then prioritize Him over our self-life. Change begins by our choosing to repent and believing in His salvation. Therefore, we are exhorted to choose, and to become a living sacrifice (Heb. 12:1). We choose to follow the drawing of the Holy Spirit within us. This affects our prioritization of His will and desire. His vision, love, and focus now become greater than our selfish self-life. Again, this needs to be balanced. Salvation should also bring blessings of joy: *"Let them shout for joy, and be glad, that favor my righteous cause: yea, let them say continually, Let the*

LORD be magnified, which hath pleasure in the prosperity of his servant" (Ps. 35:27).

Many reading this will jump for joy at the prosperity promise. Yet they will hide at the thought of prioritizing their seeking of God through prayers, devotions, and ministry to others. Our living in Christ is achieved by walking after the Spirit. Paul says, *"There is therefore now no condemnation to them which are in Christ Jesus, who walk not after the flesh, but after the Spirit"* (Rom. 8:1). The promise of no condemnation is real for those who walk after the Spirit. (Some limited Bible translations delete this condition from the promise.)

This takes a determined effort. The devil and the world always pull on our fleshly lusts. Know this: the promise of *"pleasure in the prosperity of his servant"* is genuine to *"his servant."* The question is: do we desire to serve Him with our love worship? Or do we just seek God's "sugar daddy" prosperity, heaven, and blessings in a self-life?

3. *"And every branch that bears fruit, he purges it, that it may bring forth more fruit."* We are purged (cleansed) by Holy-Word conviction. We receive revelation by the Holy Spirit and the Word (John 16:8). As we continually seek the Word, we will receive a progressive revelation of God's purposes and faithfulness. The Word is as daily manna, bringing life to our soul and spirit. When the Holy Spirit brings revelation insight, the Word becomes a hammer that forges us into combative soldier believers, each with a holy vision and purpose (Jer. 23:29). This is why Paul prayed *"that the God of our Lord Jesus Christ, the Father of glory, may give unto you the spirit of wisdom and revelation in the knowledge of him"* (Eph. 1:17).

Note: *"every branch in me"* is purged by Word revelation. The people of the world are not cleansed by the Word until they receive Christ Jesus, whom they now reject. Focus on this truth. Many languish in personal comfort while waiting for the rapture instead of joining the heart of Christ with living love. Love will birth a desire for both His Word and a burden to save the lost. The equation of loving Christ equals loving His focus: the eternal souls of man. This love promotes action. A selfish salvation is loveless and does not focus on the lost!

4. *"Now ye are clean through the word which I have spoken unto you."* The world currently refuses Christ and the cleansing by the Word. The believer "in Christ," the vine, is responsible for cleansing and taking daily showers with the Word: *"Christ also loved the church, and gave himself for it; that he might sanctify and cleanse it with the washing of water by the word"* (Eph. 5:25–26). This Word-cleansing is a responsibility shared by us and the fivefold eldership; we are responsible for maturing the church in the Word. A Word-cleansed church will be capable of ministry. They will be mature in doctrine. They will be apt to teach! (Heb. 5:12) As they pursue their personal ministry, the mature believer will capably answer the unbeliever's questions. The fivefold ministry must focus to equip believers with this vision of. This is currently not the norm, and must be changed.

5. *"Abide in me, and I in you. As the branch cannot bear fruit of itself, except it abide in the vine; no more can ye, except ye abide in me."* The world needs to be saved and become a branch grafted onto Christ, the vine. Our abiding in Christ's life is a daily holy focus, and it's much more than a Sunday religious habit. When Christians demonstrate the production of little fruit, it is due to their habits. Is there fruit? This statement is not to invoke a critical spirit, but rather a Biblical reality check. After all, Jesus Christ said, *"Ye shall know them by their fruits"* (Matt. 7:16).

   We tend to limit this to the question of if a person is saved; we must apply it to the saved who are "in Him" the vine. This speaks to the reality of the Lord dealing with the fig tree with great-looking leaves but no fruit. This good-looking tree was cursed and died an untimely death when examined "out of season." If we are a fruitful branch, Christ will never come "out of season." We need to embrace more than a Sunday religion. Fivefold ministry, when functioning and mature, will bring believers to a functional faith and fruit-bearing relationship!

6. *"I am the vine, ye are the branches: He that abides in me, and I in him, the same bring forth much fruit: for without me ye can do nothing."* We, the branches, draw life from the vine. Branches that are cut from the vine will quickly wither. When we cut ourselves off from an abiding life—a constant *"pray without ceasing"* life—our spiritual life drains

away. When life flows to us due to our abiding in the vine, we will see the fruit resulting from this life.

7. *"If a man abide not in me, he is cast forth as a branch, and withers; and men gather them, and cast them into the fire, and they are burned."* This text says what many churches and preachers fight against. Many say this being cast "into the fire" is not possible, and they avoid these scriptures. Many hold this to be an unpopular divisive subject and doctrine. Stand for this truth!

Of course, the devil wants to put believers to sleep. Of course, the devil foments bad doctrine, which is exposed by studying "all scriptures." Of course, the devil wants believers to think they have now accepted Christ, so that no matter what they do, they will possess heaven.

Rather than silencing truth, let truth be divisive. Because it exposes the great need for us to change our teaching and expectations in regards to body ministry, this text needs to be diligently weighed and preached. We are the branches in Christ, the vine. We can be removed and burned. Teaching this has made me unpopular in a few places, and greatly loved by other zealous brethren.

The truth of being a Christ servant is that I yield my person. Do not avoid this. Preach this! The result is similar to the judgment of Ananias and Sapphira. This judgment brings holy fear to where it should be (Acts 5:11). With love to all, the truth is that we either call Christ and the Holy Ghost stupid and nonsensical, or we believe His Word that we are the branches. The unsaved are not branches in Him! We, the believers in Christ, can be cut off and left to wither. Here, we are clearly told it is possible that branches in Christ can use their free will and choose to *"not abide"* in Christ, the vine; otherwise we would not be exhorted to abide in Him.

This entire teaching by our Lord centers on what our Christ-Life is. This tells us two differing results. Do we abide in Him? Either we are fruitful, or we are fruitless. Either we have a fruitful life in Christ, or we will be cut off by our Father, the heavenly gardener. If cut off, we are gathered for burning. This is the Bible-stated result of being fruitless. It affects our blessings, both now and during our eternal judgment. Who do we live for?

8. *"If ye abide in me, and my words abide in you, ye shall ask what ye will, and it shall be done unto you."* Awesome blessings come to us when we faithfully abide and seek for His Word to abide in us. I have seen the results in the lives of those who do not seek for His daily manna—those who choose to have their priorities wrong. We are responsible for maintaining devotions. We must seek a Holy-Spirit-led Christ-Life; then God's promised blessings are ours. It is our choice to dwell in the secret place of the Most High or not to (Ps. 91).

9. *"Herein is my Father glorified, that ye bear much fruit."* Many people who claim they are believers have never led a soul to Christ. Partly, this blame lies with leadership. Stop the presentation of wrong expectations to the believer body. Teach believers their responsibility, *"so shall ye be my disciples."*

We can lose our disciple status by not bearing fruit. By not maintaining our focus on His Word, our light can dim. Christ removes candlesticks as he warns the church, *"Remember therefore from whence thou art fallen, and repent, and do the first works; or else I will come unto thee quickly, and will remove thy candlestick out of his place, except thou repent"* (Rev. 2:5). Removed candles have lost their light. They did not repent or rekindle their first love for Christ. They left off being salt and light and the removal of their candlestick was their spiritual funeral and disposal.

Our first work was to repent from sin. This allowed us to enter Him, who is the door. Entering start a new life by dealing with what lies within the room beyond this door. Many want entry, but do not desire the holiness of the room within. They want fire insurance, but not to walk with Christ and the Holy Spirit. They want heaven, but they pursue a self-life. This door we entered begins a covenant faith in Christ with His love. He must be central to our daily lives. Our abiding in Christ comes to us when we prayerfully absorb daily manna. If not, it's just a matter of time until our eventual burning. Jesus said that we can lose our first love.

10. *"As the Father hath loved me, so have I loved you: continue ye in my love."* Christ's *"continue"* admonishment would not be said if it were not possible to discontinue our love. Some may find this too

confrontational. Please consider Paul's statement to the church: "*But exhort one another daily, while it is called Today; lest any of you be hardened through the deceitfulness of sin*" (Heb. 3:13). We can become hardened and return to sin. Always examine our Christ-Life and our fruit. My heart is burdened, and I weep for the many wandering, floundering, unchurched sheep who forsake assembling together.

Fivefold ministry: We can also place this blame where it rightfully belongs: in the church's ministry leadership. God speaks to this: "*Therefore so says Jehovah, the God of Israel, against the shepherds who feed My people, you have scattered My flock, and have driven them away, and have not visited them. Behold, I will bring on you the evil of your doings, says Jehovah*" (Jer. 23:2). This statement—"*have not visited them*"—is partly due to a wrong eldership structure. A functioning multiple eldership can and will visit them. We must maintain a needed personal ministry care for the flock. We must seek out the scattered.

Conclusion: Burned Branches

Recently, I read a Baptist church doctrinal document that said, "Because Christ died on the cross for our sins, there is nothing more for us to do." Many follow this horrible, unlearned thinking. All believers should be taught the truth. Do not just sit and wait for the rapture. True love for our God demands relationship fruitfulness; this is proven by our focus in life.

a) "Wherefore, *my beloved, as ye have always obeyed, not as in my presence only, but now much more in my absence,* **work out your own salvation with fear and trembling**" (Phil. 2:12). Ask yourself; why with fear unless we can fail?

b) "*Wherefore the rather, brethren, give diligence to make your calling and election sure: for if ye do these things, ye shall never fall*" (2 Pet. 1:10).

These scriptures demonstrate that we need to have more than a "fire insurance" relationship with Him, but rather a real love worship. The vine, branches, and heavenly Father dealings are a scriptural-truth presentation of our relationship with Christ. A stronger presentation of this can be studied in my manual ("Salvation Gained and Maintained with Holy Fear"). The "once saved always saved" belief is not the central theme of this writing, but it cannot be doctrinally avoided when considering the fruitfulness of a believer's ministry.

Christ-Given Talents, Expecting Fruitfulness

The results of our actions and faith will be judged and accounted for at the end of our lives, when our works will be judged by Christ upon His return. As it reads in Matthew: *"For the kingdom of heaven is as a man travelling into a far country, who called his own servants, and delivered unto them his goods. And unto one he gave five talents, to another two, and to another one; to every man according to his several ability; and straightway took his journey".* (Matt. 25:14–15)

This Christ-given teaching speaks entirely to our fruitfulness. This giving of talents by Christ, the master, is directed towards servants, and not to the unsaved world. Accolades for talents in Hollywood never equate to success in the coming judgment of Christ. The world's people are not His servants as they are gods to themselves. Those who were fruitful were told to *"enter into the joy of the Lord."* Beyond any doubt, this proves that these talented recipients were Christ-following Christians. The world is not saved by works (Eph. 2:8). Genuine Christians will demonstrate their faith by their works and life focus.

The unfaithful servants had not produced any fruit with what the Lord had given them. What have we done with what was given to us? Our Lord admonished the church (and not the world) with this exhortation: *"unto whomsoever much is given, of him shall be much required"* (Luke 12:48).

The servant who received Christ's given talents and "buried them" was rejected from *"the joy of the Lord,"* a blessed eternity. Instead, this servant was judged with: *"cast ye the unprofitable servant into outer darkness: there shall be weeping and gnashing of teeth"* (Matt. 25:30). This judgment outcome is automatic for the unsaved. The unfaithful servants, by their lack in talent usage and unfruitfulness, join this judgment of the unsaved. Fruitless servants bury what Christ gives. Preach this! Our Lord and master expects an increase and fruit from all His servants. This teaching mirrors the result of John, chapter fifteen. Fruitless branches are burned.

Faith and Continued Faithfulness

The church body needs to know what many scriptures have set out. Christ demands real fruit and love to be demonstrated by the salt-and-light ministry we are to be. Exhort those we are responsible for, AND tell them God's Word from Isaiah, the prophet: *"Esaias also cries concerning Israel, though the number of the children of Israel be as the sand of the sea, a remnant shall be saved"* (Rom. 9:27). Several million-people journeyed across the desert wasteland; all were circumcised, covenant people. All had responded to Moses: *"all the people answered together, and said, All that the LORD hath spoken we will do"* (Exod. 19:8).

Only a remnant of the Abrahamic covenant nation successfully entered the Promised Land, along with Joshua and Caleb. Many voided their circumcision (just as we void our baptism). God swore that those who did not remain faithful in their journey to the Promised Land would not be allowed to enter: *"Your fathers tempted me, proved me, and saw my works forty years. Wherefore I was grieved with that generation, and said, They do always err in their heart; and they have not known my ways. So I swore in my wrath, They shall not enter into my rest. Take heed, brethren, lest there be in any of you an evil heart of unbelief, in departing from the living God"*. (Heb. 3:9–12)

This admonishment of *"take heed brethren"* is directed to us, the church. We, just as Israel was, are on our journey to our Promised Land. We can build golden calves and depart from holiness. Now, look at how Paul relates this to us, the New Testament church of today (read all of Romans, chapters 9-11): *"Even so then at this present time also there is a remnant according to the election of grace"* (Rom. 11:5). *"A remnant."* We face the same testing on our desert journey through this world and wasteland in the shadow of death. Only the faithful, such as Joshua, Caleb, and their follower remnant, will enter into the Promised Land of rest—only those who are faithful to the end, and who maintain their first love on our journey! Paul explains that much of Israel consists of cut-off branches: *"And if some of the branches be broken off, and thou, being a wild olive tree, wert grafted in among them, and with them partake of the root and fatness of the olive tree"* (Rom. 11:17). The gospel is primarily directed to us, the gentiles, who are now being grafted into Christ the vine.

Cut-Off Branches?

A few verses later, Paul warns us about the need to be consistent in our covenant, desert journey walk: "*Well; because of unbelief they were broken off, and you stand by faith. Be not high-minded, but fear*" (Rom. 11:20). We must teach this fear; I rarely hear people teaching about holy fear in order to correct the focus of the "branches" they preach to. All of us are to be a ministering, Christ-loving people. Paul concludes this message with the main thrust of his teaching in these chapters: "*For if God spared not the natural branches, take heed lest he also spare not thee*" (Rom. 11:21). We, the New Testament gentile church, are vulnerable to not being spared. Just as the people of Israel in their journey were rejected from entering into God's rest (His Promised Land), we can fail to enter heaven.

Read this! Paul made this plain as a warning: "*lest he also spare not thee.*" Hello, church! The end of the message is: "*Behold therefore the goodness and severity of God: on them which fell, severity; but toward thee, goodness, if thou continue in his goodness: otherwise thou also shalt be cut off*" (Ro. 11:22). The Bible states that we who are grafted in "*can also be cut off.*" Preach "*IF thou continue,*" as our decision and responsibility. Preach the severity of God, as well. To continue is by us maintaining a Christ love holiness walk, "*We are made partakers of Christ, IF we hold the beginning of our confidence steadfast unto the end*" (He. 3:14).

God's Word is plain. We, just as Israel of old, can also be "*cut off*" and NOT continue in His goodness. "*If*" *we continue in His goodness, then we will not be cut off.*" If you love your people, preach this truth. Wake up your flock! God demands a genuine "first love" walk, just as He has given to us. This is proven by our conversation and actions (Mal. 3:16). God demands our continued faith and love, or else we will be subject to His righteous and severe judgment. We, the church, are responsible for what we set our hearts on: "*Set your affection on things above, not on things on the earth*" (Col. 3:2).

Today's Remnant

The apostle Paul concludes this exhortation with a somber fact that should motivate all believers to be vigilant in their Christian walk: "*Even so then, also in this present time a remnant according to the election of grace*" (Rom. 11:5). Stir up the saints we associate with. Make them aware of these scriptures! If we cannot preach remnant truth, we have a theological problem to overcome. Faith in God's Word, and love for the church, will inspire us to proclaim these severe truths, along with preaching of the blessings and God's goodness.

Born-of-the-Spirit, new-covenant people will meet God's conditions of repentance and faith with holy fear; they will have a great and humble respect for the God of Abraham, Isaac, and Jacob. We are Bible-warned. The world is told to repent and believe in order to be saved. Only believers are told "*make your election sure*" (2 Pet. 1:10). This is God's Word to you and me, the church! I weep with burden as I read and understand these words.

I know people whom I have ministered to who are baptized in the Holy Ghost and have operated in some gifts of the Spirit who today live ungodly lives. They now refute Bible truths and do not demonstrate any holy witness (Heb. 12:14). Thank God that I also know of those whom are blessed with both natural and spiritual life.

Our responsibility as an eldership and ministry leadership is to preach scriptures of God' severity and judgment, as well as the joy of heaven's reward (Lk. 6:23). This is our mandate. Our Savior spent time teaching several Bible chapters to make this point: "*For whosoever shall be ashamed of me and of my words, of him shall the Son of man be ashamed, when he shall come in his own glory, and in his Father's, and of the holy angels*" (Luke 9:26). Many people will attend church and tithe, but they will never witness to the unsaved in their work or social world. We must teach believers their ministry responsibility!

All Are a Royal Priesthood

Our Christian lives are meant to be a life of ministry; this applies to all of the body—not just a paid clergy, elders, or leaders. Peter said, "*But ye are a chosen generation, a royal priesthood, an holy nation, a peculiar people; that ye should shew forth the praises of him who hath called you out of darkness into his marvelous light*" (1 Pet. 2:9). Who does a "*royal priesthood*" refer to? "*But ye*" is the entire church and believer body that Peter addressed.

The Word comparison here is to the Levitical priesthood of the Old Testament. All Levites had a priestly ministry function. They only had one high priest, who was their chief oversight person. Now, Christ Jesus is our high priest, and His believers are a called priesthood (Heb. 8:1). He oversees our lives. He expects all of His priestly body to minister under His Lordship. When the fivefold elders mature the body for their ministry, change will come; this will only be when we prepare them by having and presenting an expectation of Biblical ministry for them.

Note that the Holy Spirit gives gifts of the Spirit to all believers who have been baptized in the Holy Ghost; however, few are encouraged and given the platform to function in them:

> *"But the manifestation of the Spirit is given to every man to profit withal. For to one is given by the Spirit the word of wisdom; to another the word of knowledge by the same Spirit; To another faith by the same Spirit; to another the gifts of healing by the same Spirit; To another the working of miracles; to another prophecy; to another discerning of spirits; to another divers kinds of tongues; to another the interpretation of tongues: But all these work by that one and the selfsame Spirit, dividing to every man severally as he will".* (1 Cor. 12:7–11)

We need to minister the baptism of the Holy Spirit to all of our believer body—those we have responsibility for. This is the first step. We need to create a worship and spiritual environment conducive to the ministry of the Spirit. Our believer gatherings should align with God's Word. We are the New Testament church; doubting this by looking at what exists instead of what should be will limit achieving a functional fivefold church.

The Bible-Ordered Church Fellowship

This is quite different from what we currently have. My heart's desire is to be linked to the heart of God. His desire is written. By faith, I see what shall be, and I strive for that. God's Word is clear in what our expectation should be when we gather: *"How is it then, brethren? When ye come together, every one of you hath a psalm, hath a doctrine, hath a tongue, hath a revelation, has an interpretation. Let all things be done unto edifying"* (1 Cor. 14:26). To achieve this liberty in fellowship gatherings, requires receiving a Holy-Word vision. This means that we must constantly work towards this. Like most apostles, I can preach three times on any and all Sundays, just as many others in the ministry can; this is the result of over forty years of ministry and my Christ-given calling. If I should seek to do this, then I will fail. I will continue to create a onefold Church.

Seeing the scriptural gathering become a reality will require encouraging fellow elders and the body to minister. Tongues, interpretation, and prophecy are more readily released in an environment of spiritual worship. Therefore, this will require times of free worship, singing in the Spirit (tongues), and with mind and thoughtful songs and prayers in worship. Teaching what 1 Corinthians, fourteen, tells us will bring understanding to the body, as to what our spiritual expectations with their participation should be. To achieve this, will require limiting some sermon time; perhaps longer "no clock" services may be in order. Release those who need to go and encourage those who can to stay. The eventual result will grow into *"every one of you has a psalm, has a doctrine, has a tongue, has a revelation, has an interpretation."* Holy order must be kept. Disallow a spiritual gifting contest, which will grieve the Holy Spirit. This scriptural gathering format will not be achieved in one day. However, when not striving for this scriptural open to "all believers" reality, this will never be.

The real question is: are we satisfied with our programmed sense of "normal"? Or do we see the scriptural possibility of *"every one of you"*? If we do not, then ask yourself, *Why not?* The scriptures speak to this! A misalignment to this New Testament church gathering expectation is wrong. This verse begins with: *"How is it then, brethren? when ye come together, every one of you hath a psalm, hath a doctrine, hath a tongue, hath a revelation, hath an interpretation"* (1 Cor. 14:26).

CHAPTER FIFTEEN:
Burden, Vision, and Fivefold Strengths

All Five Callings Are Needed

Our Lord Jesus Christ demonstrated the completion of all five callings. Upon His ascension, He gave five uniquely burdened ministry callings to mankind. When mature, all called ministries can fulfill the offices of the other four callings to some degree, but never like one specifically called to the office. Paul said, "*I magnify my office.*" He never magnified himself (Rom. 11:13). The one calling that others are limited in filling is that of the prophet, as this role requires strong revelation gifts of the Spirit. As an apostle, I have evangelized in crusade ministry. I have seen results of souls being saved and healed; however, there is a unique anointing and greater ministry result when a called evangelist ministers at a crusade.

Some of us have experienced a prophet trying to pastor a church with limited pastoral results. They can function in this office, but only to a limited degree; they do not have the wiring to be very successful. Their results while pastoring will involve a greater impartation of revelation gifts among the flock; however, patient, heartfelt burden-bearing and counseling will be limited.

All of the genuine gift callings receive differing heart burdens, and they differ in their ministry vision as they mature. Just like an electrician runs particular wiring in a house, or a mechanic in a car, the Holy Spirit likewise molds the callings with different "wirings" and strengths.

Sadly, we see much of the world's evangelism and the harvest being lost due to not having a unified and functional fivefold gift ministry. Many believers—especially the newly born ones—are malnourished due to not having a multiple ministry eldership to nurture them. Thus, many are babies that are brought to birth, but left to die. This results in what our Savior said: *"And these are they likewise which are sown on stony ground; who, when they have heard the word, immediately receive it with gladness; And have no root in themselves, and so endure but for a time: afterward, when affliction or persecution arises for the word's sake immediately they are offended".* (Mark 4:16–17) All babes need care.

A caring, shepherding, multiple eldership will see to it that roots of knowledge and faith grow as they care for these infants (Mark 4:17). The pastor-only ministry cannot effectively do what the multiple eldership can. A diet of Sunday morning praise and sermon will never achieve this growth of care; however, a released multiple eldership ministry will.

The Apostle

When mature, the apostle is much more than a "sent-out" ministry, as some claim. The apostle has an overseeing placement with a governmental ministry. In time, they guide churches and raise up other ministries, and they will have a heart and discernment ability that will enable them to raise up multiple elders in all churches. When mature and of a right spirit, the apostle has a Christ-mandated, first-place governmental authority in church ministry: *"And God has set some in the church, first apostles"* (1 Cor. 12:28). This is fought against by most churches and ministries who are in charge today. Such churches and ministries will fight to maintain a first-place control and ignore the discerning of Christ's ministry setting order; instead, they establish their own setting. Should apostles enter their domain, they immediately view them as competition. These churches and ministries should carefully discern other Christ-given callings, just as all true shepherds should. What is the character, ministry calling, and the focus of ministry guests? Onefold blindness is rampant.

In our dealings with fellow ministries, always remember that all ministries can fail and be of a wrong spirit. The apostle, Judas, went astray with wrong-heartedness (Acts 1:25). He was just as much a called apostle as Peter and Paul were, who both had tremendous ministries. Jesus sent Judas out as a miracle ministry on His behalf (Mark 6:7–13). Judas' failure was due to not overcoming sin. He retained a covetous heart *"because*

he was a thief, and had the bag, and bare what was put therein" (John
12:6). Apostle Paul knew this truth and with humility said: *"I keep under
my body, and bring it into subjection: lest that by any means, when I have
preached to others, I myself should be a castaway"* (1 Cor. 9:27; Gal. 6:1).

Apostles, due to their larger, Holy-Ghost-given world ministry vision,
may succumb to pride and impatience and flaunt their authority with a
spirit of control. Just like all ministry callings, they can become money-
focused, justifying themselves by seeing the supposed good due to their
ministry pursuits. A right-hearted apostle and all ministries should have
a father's heart for the believers and churches. When a mature apostle
functions with the right spirit, a gift miracle and healing ministry normally occurs. Genuine apostles will be exceptional in their doctrinal
focus (1 Tim. 4:6).

I get a holy anger when people and women, who claim to be apostles
entitle themselves as "chief apostles." This self-image focus interferes with
humility, Bible truth, and godliness.

Apostles and Denominations

In 2016, for the first time in twenty-five years, while looking to gain
insight from what other ministries project, I purchased a couple of books
focused on fivefold ministry. I had previously resisted doing so to avoid
being tainted by humanistic thoughts versus the pure Word of God's revelation. I also know that no one has all knowledge.

One of the two books I purchased was a compilation by several contributors. The foreword was by a blessed Matthew Greene, the editor of a
Christian magazine. This book, entitled *Understanding Fivefold Ministry*,
contains a lot of ministry insight that all can learn from. However, it
became evident that not one of the contributors was an apostle; none
spoke of the apostle's wiring or ministry fruit with understanding. None
withstood some of the content in this book that any apostle should
understand and correct. The foreword was written by Jack Hayford, a
now-deceased minister.

Without doing a complete critique on this writing and while wanting
to be respectful, Pastor Jack limits his apostle's view to "one being sent
out." He did not touch apostle truths. He did not mention apostle

governmental authority or their gifted doctrinal focus. Many pastor ministries preach their authority to their leadership while being incapable of
coming under the authority of Christ. They disregard the "set some" and
Christ given apostles, prophets, and teachers.

Pastors are wired to be pastors; they are not Holy-Ghost-wired as
apostles. Pastors are not given the Holy Ghost's burden and vision of an
apostle or prophet. Pastors should kneel to God's Word and seek out the
leading and inclusion of apostles in their ministry. They should believe in
an apostle-led, Christ-desired government. Faith in God's Word regarding this must be obeyed.

Destroy unbelief. The Word says, "*And God hath set some in the church,
first apostles, secondarily prophets, thirdly teachers*" (1 Cor. 12:28). Faith in
this scripture precedes all other understandings of authority. Faith says,
"God said it, so I believe and want to humbly establish this and submit
to this."

Apostle understanding and wiring will not be gained from this book,
"Understanding Fivefold Ministry". Matthew Green and Jack Hayford,
contributors to this book are ministry who do not understand this
subject. Mathew and Jack disregard and are limited in understanding of
governmental burden, vision, and authority. This is a burden and Christ-
given insight into the genuine apostle. When a book says that "there are
some advantages that a denomination has in comparison to apostle-led
fivefold churches," this indicates an equally good acceptance of what the
onefold-pastor-led denominational system projects.

By this, the genuine fivefold scriptural ministry is denied. This is the
very system that lacks revelation and needs renovation. We decry the
wrongness of this. Change this system that destroys the honoring of
Christ's giving. Any church ministry structure that denies the Christ-
given church government setting is lacking: "*And God hath set some in
the church, first apostles, secondarily prophets, thirdly teachers, after that
miracles*" (1 Cor. 12:28).

There is no doubt in my mind that denominational structures were
and are well-intended; they just lack scriptural insight. I also know
that you cannot teach the unteachable. Regardless, thank God for all

Christ-seeking-churches, as salvation does go forth. As good as this may be, scriptural ignorance does not justify our lack of obedience.

No calling will understand the loss and hampering of the gospel that's occurring in the world due to the unbelief and rejection of the apostle, prophet, and teacher as much as the apostle will. Disobedience brings great damage to world church establishing. The ministries who do not discern the given multiple callings often reject others due to a spirit of competition. They ruin the Christ-given, unified flow and functioning of the five given callings. When other Christ appointed ministry arise in their midst, they manipulate them to leave, rather than incorporate them into a collegial ministry.

Holy-Ghost-Inspired Ministry

The posturing of "have faith, go and start a different church of your own" is common. Sometimes, this is due to not understanding the differences between callings. More often, it is a preservation of their financial positioning. Many wrongfully view a working ministry as immature; they should be viewed as a mature servanthood. Those who hold this critical opinion usually receive ministry remuneration while being blind to the needs of fellow elders.

An apostle-led church with genuine apostles' honors and encourages all callings.

The denial of Christ's setting in church ministry—even if it is well intended—places us and our ministries as wiser than God! (Isa. 55:8) Obedience to His Word is true worship. Samuel told stubborn and prideful King Saul the truth, *"Samuel said, Hath the LORD as great delight in burnt offerings and sacrifices, as in obeying the voice of the LORD? Behold, to obey is better than sacrifice, and to hearken than the fat of rams. For rebellion is as the sin of witchcraft, and stubbornness is as iniquity and idolatry"*. (1 Sam. 15:22–23)

Ignoring God's will by not honoring His giving and His governmental placing is stubborn disobedience "as witchcraft." Good intentions do not justify other untruthful, counterfeit ministry structures. Denominational structures were well intended to safeguard doctrinal beliefs. This guarded the church from past wrong errors. However, when these beliefs limit what Christ Jesus said through newly gleaned scriptural revelation, then receive change.

Increased revelation will demonstrate God's will. We must always be open to changing our views and theology when Word revelation shows correction and light. When we do not understand the "why" of His government setting, we must seek to understand it. He will give an increase of understanding to the obedient and seeking.

Disobedience causes us to become an enemy to Christ's ministry, His giving, and His setting. Good intentions, with an avoidance of what Christ Jesus desires, is not just a denial of His Word, but also of His Lordship. His setting is, *"God hath set some in the church, first apostles, secondarily prophets, thirdly teachers."* This denial starts with those who deny and place limited value on the gift of tongues and the baptism of the Holy Spirit. Then it goes on from there.

All existing denominations limit a multiple ministering eldership, including the five Christ-given callings. Unless genuine apostles are discerned and given a ministry platform, we will have a continually rebellious onefold church, resulting in a huge ongoing loss for the Kingdom of God.

The genuine apostle has a larger vision of souls and churches being established in unconquered territory. They will love the home church they establish and encourage, but they will also have a burden and vision for seeing how other new churches rise up by gathering many new souls. They will cherish the valued blessings of all called ministries in this pursuit.

The Apostle's Heart, Calling, and Ministry

At the end of His earthly ministry, our Lord addressed the eleven apostles he had raised up: *"Then the eleven disciples went away into Galilee, into a mountain where Jesus had appointed them"* (Matt. 28:16). Here we see what attends the heart of genuine apostles, when Jesus said to them, *"Go ye therefore, and teach all nations"* (Matt. 28:19). The Lord still gives the church apostles and prophets. They will always have a desire to reach nations other than their home church. When Paul visited Jerusalem, all of the eleven original apostles went to differing territories, as history supports; only the apostle James, the Lord's brother, who was not of the eleven, was in Jerusalem with Peter (Gal. 1:19).

The pastor has not been given this "heart wiring," nor should they, as their wiring is for their local flock. The painful error is when the pastor denies and does not uphold the apostle's wiring. They thereby limit the ministry of Christ. When they deny the "apostle first" rule of Christ's given setting, by ignorance or wrong-heartedness, they bring destruction to the world church ministry. They also limit the apostle's strengths, which are Christ-given, by ignoring the apostle's unique, Holy-Spirit wiring. This wiring would benefit their church people. Whether by ego (that is, demanding and defending a "first-place" authority placement) or by ignorance, their denial of the apostle's placement and ministry brings destruction to what Christ legislates. Christ Jesus has told us His setting in place, how the church government is to function. This given structure is now denied (1 Co. 12:28)!

We must be careful to not take a calling title that does not belong to us. If one takes the title of a calling, that person must take the burden of the Lord and walk with the responsibility that comes with the calling. They must walk in obedience to His mandate, and with humility. The real apostle's heart is glimpsed in what Paul wrote when he addressed the Corinthian church: "*As touching our brother Apollos, I greatly desired him to come unto you with the brethren: but his will was not at all to come at this time; but he will come when he shall have convenient time*" (1 Cor. 16:12). Here we see:

a) A love for the church of Corinth, which was not the apostle's home base of Antioch. As well we see the apostle's heart of seeing their need of knowledge, with his burden to strengthen and safeguard them;
b) Paul's "father's heart" in the words "*I greatly desired*," which speaks of his deep care;
c) Paul's esteeming of the ministry strength of other callings, like the teacher, Apollos;
d) Paul's mutual accountability as he surrenders to Apollos' choice of time to attend Corinth with a demonstrated lack of a spirit of control.

The functional fivefold church will understand that mutual esteeming and accountability means being submissive to Christ. They accept the honored Christ-given ministry of fellow ministries. Apostles will rejoice in seeing their Timothies and other ministries flow in their holy callings. They know that all churches need a multiple ministering eldership, and that all churches are "out of order" without this (Titus 1:5). This is the real start to honoring fivefold Bible truth! Anyone claiming to be an apostle (there's questionably too many) who does not have a great burden for believers to be established in sound doctrine tells me that they are not apostles. Sound doctrine is a natural and strong Holy-Ghost wiring that comes with the calling (Titus 1:9).

Apostles always have a greater governmental wiring burden. Prophets are limited in this. All prophets should recognize the Christ given priority placement of apostles. Apostles act as a constant Bible school by raising up other ministries (Acts 13:13, 16:1, 21:8).

The apostle's heart will always desire to see churches blessed by the covenant ministries they have relationships with (Phil. 2:19, 25; 1 Cor. 16:12). They will have a bonding with numerous other ministries as part of their normal heart focus (Col. 4:7–18; 1 Co. 16:17–19).

Apostle Recognition Is a Must

When we don't recognize apostles, the damage to the Kingdom is incalculable. When genuine apostles are honored and given their rightful "first-place" function, the Christian world outreach and the establishment of churches will excel; this is an apostle's Holy-Spirit-given vision and burden. A pastor does not prioritize this vision, but this is not wrong! Pastors are not given this priority focus in their wiring; instead, they correctly focus on their local flock. They are wrong when they do not receive and respect the apostle and other callings. When apostles are set free to function, they will:

a) Discern Holy-Spirit-called potential ministries (Acts 16:3);
b) Wholeheartedly do their all to mentor and bring ministries to a functional maturity (Acts 16:1–3; Titus 3:7);

c) Encourage the ministry of the saints (currently, this is not prioritized) (Heb. 5:12);

d) Focus strongly on setting the church government and elders in place to oversee and protect the churches (Titus 1:5; Acts 20:28);

e) React to wrong beliefs with boldness, establishing gospel truth in the face of error with doctrinal strength (Acts 19:1–6; Gal. 2:11, 3:1; 1 Tim. 1:10; Titus 2:1);

f) Confront, judge, and deal with wrongdoing in order to maintain a holy church for the good of all, protection of the flock and the those in error (1 Cor. 5:1);

g) Honor and encourage strengthening by all the other called ministries they are involved with, especially those whom they oversee (1 Cor. 16:12; Phil. 2:19, 25);

h) encourage seeking spiritual gifts, as well as the releasing of these gifts in body ministry (Rom. 1:11; 1 Cor. 14:1);

i) In maturity, with Holy-Spirit anointing, impart gifts of the Spirit (1 Tim. 4:14);

j) Teach holy financial principles (Acts 20:33–35; 1 Cor. 9:11–12; 2 Cor. 12:18);

k) Teach a servant ministry's focus (Jude 1:1; James 1:1; Gal. 5:13; Eph. 4:16);

l) Focus on Christ and not on themselves (1 Cor. 11:1, 2:2; Rom. 1:4);

m) contend for and establish sound doctrine, thereby safe-guarding the churches;

The result of their functional ministry (when mature and godly) will be the establishment of a world church empowered by tremendous growth, and anointing power with miracles.

The Prophet and Prophetess

I see many confused prophets or prophetesses erroneously claim-ing to be apostles in their calling. This is due to some common vision factors that the apostles share. They will have a larger-than-local church vision. Often, their stationary logo will be a global picture of the world. However, they will lack the apostle's deep burden, doctrine focus, and ability to establish church eldership and government. They are rightfully a "foundation ministry." The church is built on the foundation of both the apostles and prophets: *"upon the foundation of the apostles and prophets, Jesus Christ Himself being the chief cornerstone"* (Eph. 2:20). The apostles and prophets will establish hearing and safeguarding in direction. They will focus on holiness: a treasured truth. Honor them as they operate in the gifts of revelation and power. All prophets rightfully love what their Holy-Ghost-wiring brings them to; they love to get under the anointing in gatherings, or a worshipping music flow that enhances Holy Spirit presence. They want to hear the voice of the Holy Spirit and minister that. They want all believers to hear the voice of God. When I see ministries holding meetings with a focus of worship and presence, they are usually led by prophet callings.

The prophet's wiring focuses on "hearing, discerning, and presence." Genuine prophets and prophetesses will have a deep burden for all believers to hear the voice of God. To minister in the revelation gifts is a heavenly joy to them, and to the recipients, as well.

There are differing flavors among the prophet's (or prophetess') ministries. We also have the "intercessory" prophets who receive in-depth prayer and Holy-Spirit-directed burdens. These burdens may be for churches, individuals, or families. They are the "watchmen on the wall" and are of huge value, as they discern danger and enemy strategies. Dreams and visions are common to them. All will have a natural desire and inner knowledge that they will minister in places other than just their home church; when they are faithful, the Lord will bring them to do this.

Their message while speaking will focus on presence, holiness, and godly principles. They tend to be black and white with little room for gray in their insights. Unlike the apostle, they rarely press into a strong doctrinal or governmental focus. They are weak in raising up elders, but strong in imparting revelation gifts, raising up other prophetic believers.

Irreplaceable and Incomparable Prophet Ministry

When the prophet ministry is mature and received by the churches, the strengthening and encouraging by their ministry and gifting is profound. Receive and honor them:

a) The prophetic ministry has discerning spiritual eyes to see what others do not see.

b) Their strengthening of the ministry's hands and believer body is profound. Churches are weakened by a huge loss when they don't receive this calling. When this is the case, they deny the truth that all believers should be baptized in the Holy Ghost. All believers should minister in some gifts of the Spirit and edify the body (1 Cor. 12:11; Eph. 4:16).

c) The genuine prophet calling will teach holiness, just as the apostles also will. Prophets know our God is holy. They understand presence anointing. They know and teach that holiness is the door for people to enter into His holy manifest presence.

d) The prophet calling will seek and bring down anointing presence to the body.

e) Prophet callings vary greatly in their gifts and strengths. Some are very strong in giving Holy Spirit revelation personal prophetic words, while others are an intercessory revelation gift ministry with a limited personal prophesying ministry. Regardless of what branch of prophecy they operate in, they are a huge Christ-given blessing. My ministry friend of forty years is a Jonah-messenger-type prophet. His focus is intercessory prayer. Prophets will receive prophetic insight of coming events. My intercessory prophetess wife sees coming events with dreams, visions, and sometimes "open visions." The prophet Agabus visited Antioch and prophetically told them to prepare for a severe coming drought which occurred shortly after (Acts 11:28). All churches should be blessed with prophet ministry.

f) They defend against negative spiritual strategies.

g) I find their weakness is receiving correction, due to their gifts and a pride of calling.

The Teacher

The Christ-appointed teacher, like Apollos, will be strong in the scriptures (Acts 18:24). The teacher's focus and burden will be to impart knowledge to the believing church. As an elder, they will have a pastoral burden for the believer body, but they will be limited in the burden-bearing role of pastoral work. They do not carry the evangelistic fervor of the evangelist. They are not heavily wired for these functions. Give them a hungry, believing assembly, and they are in their cup of joy as they teach and impart knowledge. They constantly have a burden of "if the people only knew." Their teachings are more than a message of faith or comfort. The matured teacher will have an in-depth, Word- food-giving, Word-revelation ability.

If the "pastoring" ministry in a church is a called evangelist, the focus will be salvation. People will hunger for more than just a salvation message. A teacher will satisfy this as they expound on teaching themes and series regarding multiple truths. Usually they have the apostle's teaching ability, but not their burden for teaching doctrine or raising up elders,

Strengthening by the Teacher

Just as a mature apostle will have a burden for world ministry and church establishment, by comparison, the teacher has a burden of knowledge impartation. This may not be to a singular church, but rather to churches. Apollos traveled. People are limited in their personal growth when all they hear is a focus on faith, comfort, or evangelism. The teacher will dig into detailed meanings of Old- and New-Testament truth treasures, setting these out with depth.

Apollos was a great Biblical example of this. He was not introduced to us with an evangelist's focus, as Phillip was. He was not assigned to set elders in place, as the young apostles Timothy and Titus were. He was not known for a gifting-and-strengthening prophet ministry, as the prophet Agabus was. He was not a stationary ministry, which is how a pastor would be focused. However, his calling is third in governmental authority. This is due to his Christ- and Holy-Spirit-given burden to impart depth in Bible teaching and knowledge. God-given knowledge is a holy insurance policy against perishing. Their focus is different from what a pastor excels in—which is the shepherding and care of people with loving them through difficulties in life's complexities (Hosea 4:6).

The Pastor

The called pastor will have a message of faith and comfort. In maturity, they will also have strong doctrinal understanding but will focus more on believer encouragement messages. Their church is their entire ministry world. They have the least amount of desire of all the five callings to travel and minister elsewhere. With joy, they will see new believer salvations occur, but that is not their main wiring focus. Rather, the safety and welfare of the local flock is their correct Holy Spirit prioritized wiring in their ministry walk.

They will be keen to defend the flock and see that wolves are kept out. They will easily discern if people are in need or care. As an anchor ministry, pastors will more readily build and strengthen a cohesive church body. Godly pastors will not defer from kneeling before Christ and His Lordship. When they do, they will accept the "first" in governmental ministry placement of the apostle, then prophet, and teacher. They will seek understanding of the Christ-given s multiple callings. All of the callings are to fulfill church building ministry. When they accept Christ's giving of the five callings, world-conquering church building will prosper.

The Pastor's Burden-Bearing Strength

The Christ-given calling of our beloved pastors lies in the consistent, sheep-caring strength they are endowed with. Carrying both young or mature in their hearts. This is a unique strength given to all genuine pastors. Isaiah said this of our master shepherd: "*He shall feed his flock like a shepherd: he shall gather the lambs with his arm, and carry them in his bosom, and shall gently lead those that are with young*" (Isa. 40:11). No elder or other ministry member will have the sheep-caring ability or the heart of the beloved pastor.

Pastors have a protective, people-discerning eye. More than the other callings, they will hurt for the hurt and weep with the weeping. They rejoice with the rejoicing. Among the elders, they are an anchor ministry to the local flock. Believe God's Word. Christ says that pastors are not first, second, or third in the ministry's authority placement; pastors disregarding this will limit Christ in church building.

The Evangelist

Just as a hungry man desires food, a genuine evangelist is hungry for souls. Their exceptional burden and wired vision is to save the lost. They have a strong Holy-Spirit wiring that causes them to see and reveal the reality of hell and damnation. They see both the glory of heaven and the devastation of hell to be attained or avoided through the power of the cross. Salvation versus damnation of the lost is a constant burden for the evangelist. Within the church, they will constantly motivate the believer body to do evangelistic outreach; this is so greatly needed.

Evangelists will build a church in numbers faster than any other callings. However, in time, the church will tire due to lacking and needed in-depth teaching. They will hunger for Word truths, along with greater "elder care." People need more than salvation and a faith-focused message. They will be prone to eventually leaving in search for a different believer body. They hunger for more and different Word food. Real believers have a natural hunger for the Christ-intended banquet table. Evangelists mature the church by imparting a vision for salvation of souls. In church building, they need the other callings to come alongside and care for the newly saved.

The evangelist Philip had a tremendous healing and miracle ministry (a common strength in the mature members of this calling). Others came alongside them and contributed with their ministry to the new converts (Acts 8:14). The beauty of the evangelist burden, more than any other calling, is their burning zeal and anointing to see souls know salvation through the gospel. They confront man. They preach that man must know Christ Jesus (Acts 8:5).

Their message will present Kingdom of God truths, while also presenting repentance (Matt. 4:17). Most are limited in in-depth Bible doctrinal teachings (Acts 8:12). Others are wrong if they think the evangelist's preaching is shallow. Their Christ message will focus on the coming judgment of all mankind before our holy God. They will preach that all are welcomed to receive redemption through the cross. All can avoid an eternal hell by turning from sin to salvation by believing in Christ Jesus and His cross-purchased redemption.

In the church body, they will always focus the believers on soul winning. They preach hell fires and judgment awaiting those without Christ. They have a unique holy impartation that brings conviction to people as they preach. Also, the mature evangelist will function in a ministry of miracles and healing, which confirms their preaching (Acts 8:6; Mark 16:17).

Evangelists will not be strong in presenting doctrine when compared to the apostle or teacher. They will not be as strong in shepherding, counseling, and burden-bearing as the pastor; compared to the pastor, they are also weak in prophetic matters.

Elder Ministry

The elder ministry is a key and much-needed topic to understand in fivefold church building. Doctrinally, let us begin with the following: "*This is a true saying, If a man desire the office of a bishop, he desires a good work*" (1 Tim. 3:1). Most elders are not of the five ascension gift callings (1 Tim. 3:1). They are raised up and matured by the Holy Spirit in their burden and vision to feed and oversee the flock (Acts 20:17, 28). They will be limited unless fellow elders humbly see this scriptural truth. Make room and encourage them in ministry.

The terms "bishop," "overseer," and "elder" describe the same ministry office with a different functional expression. The Ephesus elders are named "overseers" (Acts 20:17, 28). The elders that Titus was to ordain were referred to as "bishops" when their qualifications were set out (Titus 1:5, 7). For a comparison, consider how a business owner may also be called a "manager."

In building a fivefold church, we rarely have all the five callings simultaneously available and at home. All should be part of a home base with an overseeing apostle. In larger established fivefold churches—such as the Bible's Jerusalem church after Pentecost, with thousands attending—probably all of the ministry callings were present. Today this is unusual as I know of no large full gospel Fivefold church that genuinely functions with a multiple eldership fivefold callings ministry. Many may not be present, as they will travel to minister elsewhere. Due to this, the eldership who are not of the fivefold callings are more prone to do pastoral visitation and personal care work. Although they may not be of a Christ-appointed pastor calling, all elders do shepherd.

All elders are to oversee and feed by imparting teaching and Word truths. All need to be involved in overseeing the flock. This is what the Holy Spirit has prepared them for: "*Take heed therefore unto yourselves, and to all the flock, over the which the Holy Ghost hath made you overseers, to feed the church of God*" (Acts 20:28).

Question the Truth of Functional Elders

Functional eldership is a key priority and an important subject to understand and apply. It involves the elder ministry to the flock. In many larger churches, although they have "elders," the lack of elder functioning can be observed in the following scenarios:

a)   the main speaker during Sunday services is a onefold, singular person (while supposedly seeking fivefold ministry);

b)   families and single people can miss services and nobody seems to notice;

c)   visitors and seekers can flow in and out with no one knowing who they are; and

d)   membership families and single people can exist an entire year and not have a personal elder visitation with a spiritual focus for guidance and input.

God's Complaint of His Ministry Due to Denial of Plural elder Shepherds

Our God's complaint to shepherds (with an included judgment) is the following: "*Woe be unto the pastors that destroy and scatter the sheep of my pasture! says the LORD. Therefore so says Jehovah, the God of Israel, against the shepherds who feed My people, You have scattered My flock, and have driven them away, and not visited them*" (Jer. 23:1–2). Note that this is spoken to shepherds "*who feed My people.*" This is spoken to shepherds who preach and teach while ministering on the Sabbath day. They fulfilled a called position. This statement involves God's complaint against the pastors who "*have . . . not visited them*." This is a strong truth we need to address in our churches here and now.

This none personal visiting by ministry is a key matter to be understood; then we must implement a correction for this lack. This speaks to our caring for the flock in relational matters. Only by mature (or maturing) personal elder visitations will this lack be remedied. We need multiple ordained elders. God says that the result of not visiting the flock results in the following: "*You have scattered My flock, and have driven them away*"! No bonding relationships occur, no personal, heart-level care from elders to people in spiritual matters.

Preaching at people versus visiting is very different. The spiritual status of our people must be discerned. An apostle—or any solo onefold ministry—cannot achieve a close, caring, and personal relational knowledge of people unless the church is small.

A multiple eldership can minister, bond, and care for the people; they can personally know them over a period of time. Personal visitation is required to encourage and discern where the people are at in their walk with the Lord. Multiple elders must minister discerning the needs of the flock; they must learn where people are spiritually. What the Holy Spirit is doing in their lives to encourage them? We must promote the elders' ministry. This is the reality of (Act 2:42), "*they continued in the apostle's doctrine and fellowship*".

Elder Care

Everyone needs personal elder care; that is, a relationship with a genuine, right-hearted, and knowledgeable elder—one or more elders who will know them, pray with them, and be a sounding board for their focus. That is true shepherding, and it goes far beyond attending services. The elders take responsibility for their personal spiritual care and needs, but never from a controlling position. "Caring for" involves the flock we oversee. It only applies to those whom the Lord admonishes: "*Obey them that have the rule over you, and submit yourselves: for they watch for your souls, as they that must give account, that they may do it with joy, and not with grief: for that is unprofitable for you*" (Heb. 3:17). Our responsibility to the church flock involves elder care with a close spiritual relationship with our flock.

Real concern for the flock means caring while sharing. This is a heart-to-heart matter of ministering with loving wisdom. Eldership is a relational involvement in spiritual ministry—a loving, parental, and spiritual care. It enables elders to bring in personal encouragement and direction while mentoring. When eldership engages in fulfilling God's care of having "*visited them*," there will be much growth in all involved—both the elders and the people.

Again, it takes wisdom and planning to cover all of the people. Some of the flock will have a preference for specific elders; we must allow for this. This is where we must put to death a spirit of competition. This is where we must esteem fellow elders. We thereby encourage others to fulfill their elder's qualifications while employing what all elders must be: "*apt to teach* and be hospitable" (1 Tim. 3:2).

Eldership ministry under God is a matter of continual growth. It involves teaching knowledge, wisdom, and spiritual principles. It must not become our taking of a wrongful, controlling position. Some ministry took this position during a past "shepherding movement." God sets people free, and we must also. God despises a control focus.

To make personal elder visitation godly and honorable, a responsible ministry body must honor the eldership before the gathered assembly. They are God's holy ministry servants!

The Christ-Given Five Callings: Team Strengths

By reasoning away and harboring a disbelief of Christ's giving, the devil has gained in his destruction. By us being faithful believers in God's Holy Word, the restoration of the five given callings will be discerned and restored. When the fivefold government of God is flowing together with a mutual esteeming, great things will happen. Real growth will take place. The effect on world evangelism will be powerful. Unlike today, where the church consists of thousands of uncoordinated Christian guerilla groups, we will become a cohesive army. When we have the team strengths of unity and unyielding fervor, we will establish what is written.

Restoring the Church

Restoring the church involves the strong discerning, acceptance, and implementing of truths. We must:

1. Discern the differing callings, those who are genuinely called and appointed by Christ.
2. Seek an understanding of the reasons for the first, second, and third authority order.
3. Honor Christ and His Lordship by determining to establish this.
4. Know those who are of the five callings can be of a wrong spirit, with unholy failures.
5. Extend them grace, by allowing them to grow while confronting any failures.
6. Understand that all called ministry are intended to be elders when they are mature.
7. Know that all elders will be expected to be released into visible ministry functions.
8. Honor "any man" elders, who are not of the five-gift callings (1 Tim. 3:1).
9. Understand and implement New Testament financial dealings and principles.
10. Have a strong focus on acquiring unity in doctrine (1 Cor. 1:10).
11. Change our understanding; promote and honor ministry by the body. This includes the holy recognition of the "marketplace," Christian businessmen. Their financial ministry is a holy endeavor before the Lord. They bring church provision by their ministry.

Failure and Kingdom Loss

We must discern and correct the wrong calling identifications that currently exist. When we are wrong in our discernment of the callings, we sow confusion, thereby obscuring the real callings. Much damage is being done due to this. Our Lord places great importance on the exactness of His giving the callings.

We should never succumb to the lust of desiring to look like some other calling than what is Christ given to us. Usually, this error is birthed when we desire the accolades of man, rather than what Jesus Christ has called us to be. Wait on the Lord. Weigh in your own heart what your ministry burden is, and then follow a vision of how to attain it.

Even in Old Testament teachings, King Uzziah failed in this. He was a blessed and godly king for many years. Pride entered and, "*when he was strong, his heart was lifted up to his destruction: for he transgressed against the LORD his God, and went into the temple of the LORD to burn incense upon the altar of incense*" (2 Chron. 26:16). He took the duty that only belonged to the Levitical priesthood calling upon himself; this calling was not his. The priesthood under Azzariah tried to stop him, but to no avail. This resulted in the following: "*Then Uzziah was wroth, and had a censer in his hand to burn incense: and while he was wroth with the priests, the leprosy even rose up in his forehead before the priests in the house of the LORD, from beside the incense altar*" (2 Chron. 26:19).

Now consider the importance that God places on the correctness of callings, as well as the Kingdom loss that currently exists by denial of some callings. Christ-appointed apostles are needed to lead and be first in His church's governmental order: "*And God hath set some in the church, first apostles, secondarily prophets, thirdly teacher*" (1 Cor. 12:28). At this time, most churches, by man's ignorance, have placed named pastors first, even though they may be of a different calling. Determined faith and obedience will correct this!

Church Ministry Government: Truth Conclusion

When called ministry do not recognize or seek out the apostle's oversight and inclusion in their ministry, they are "OUT OF ORDER," just like churches are without a multiple eldership. Those who are ignorant of this scriptural authority, as set out by our Lord, need to repent and humbly seek out the scriptures regarding this matter. Those who know that the Word says this, but do not want to submit to the apostle's oversight are rebellious to Christ. Our Lord gives and sets differing callings in the church. Ministry who deny this place limitations on their personal spiritual potential because of ignoring this.

Due to the errors of some apostles of today (just like Judas in Christ's day), many will excuse away Christ's setting of authority. Many people justify their rebellion by rationalizing away Holy Scriptures.

Those who ignore the need for the authority placements of the prophet and teacher callings are acting in ignorance and rebellion. Humility and godly obedience will bring an increase to your ministry. The following scriptures are a few that speak to this truth:

a) *"A high look, and a proud heart, and the plowing of the wicked, is sin"* (Prov. 21:4).

b) *"Hear ye, and give ear; be not proud: for the LORD hath spoken"* (Jer. 13:15).

c) *"Do ye think that the scripture says in vain, the spirit that dwells in us lusts to envy? But he giveth more grace. Wherefore he says, God resists the proud, but giveth grace unto the humble"* (Jms. 4:5–6).

d) *"Humble yourselves therefore under the mighty hand of God, that he may exalt you in due time"* (1 Pet. 5:6). When we consider submission and authority involvements, do not just think of authority. Look for the benefits of Christ's wisdom, His giving, that bring improvements to us and the church through the strengths of all callings. By our obedience, we glorify Him. Growth in church ministry will be huge and widespread as we receive the strengths of the different callings!

CHAPTER 16:
A Functioning Fivefold Ministry

Multiple Eldership:

My first Philippines fivefold ministry leadership conference was in 1991 with my covenant apostle, Ernesto Balili. Since then, the Lord has confirmed to me through a strong visitation and holy presence that His church will be restored—that is, an operational church established with fivefold knowledge and principles. There are applicable truths we must know. The first is that all elders must be both hospitable and apt to teach. We must understand that all five callings and elders must be upheld. We must encourage and uphold all of them in our ministry to the people.

All of the eldership is to focus on bringing the church assembly to maturity; this will be seen by the ministry of the church body. Are they? All elders are also to be released as they act out their vision and ministry using their knowledge. We bring children to birth, but we must also have an equal heart to bring them to maturity. This will require scheduling weeknight study times. Have dialoging to become of one mind, with open discussion as a teaching format. This will promote unity among our church family (1 Cor. 1:10).

Those we oversee must understand Christ's giving: "*We beseech you, brethren, to know them which labor among you, and are over you in the Lord, and admonish you*" (1 Thess. 5:12). All Christ-given callings are needed and are part of "*them which labor among you.*"

We see this example by Paul: "*from Miletus he sent to Ephesus, and called the elders of the church*" (Acts 20:17). All were recognized as elders, regardless of their callings. Paul, in his discourse, did not separate them from a common responsibility: "*the Holy Ghost hath made you overseers, to feed the church of God*" (Acts 20:28). To accept anything less in our churches is a willful denial of God's Word. It will take humility from all servant hearted ministry to make this a reality.

The New Testament ministries usually identified themselves by their calling. This was not being prideful, but a clarification of their calling. To wit, I am a plumber and not a roofer.

The Functioning

More is said about the apostle ministry in New Testament writings than any other calling. Why is this? Perhaps this is because when we allow this calling to rise, then all of the callings will also rise and function. If we could seek out, encourage, and allow apostles to function, then all of the other callings would be upheld and released with a greater fruitfulness. Mature apostles strongly desire all callings to function—not just their personal ministry. This, of course, has other factors involved. Let us review both the good and the bad of these.

My heart leaps with joy when I see the history of Paul meeting Timothy. Paul eagerly discerns the hand of God upon this young man. Then he determines to train him in ministry by taking him along in his ministry travels, "*Then came he to Derbe and Lystra: and, behold, a certain disciple was there, named Timotheus, the son of a certain woman, which was a Jewess, and believed; but his father was a Greek: Which was well reported of by the brethren that were at Lystra and Iconium. Him would Paul have to go forth with him*". (Acts 16:1–3)

This wonderful picture represents the flow of what can and should be. The apostle's discernment of this young called ministry caused Paul to respond with a mentoring and fatherly heart. He was willing to pour knowledge and spiritual principles into Timothy as they spent time together. This travel involved endless hours of mentoring, reasoning, and an impartation of ministry experience. Paul did not say that Timothy should attend a Bible school somewhere; he *was* the Bible school.

There was no local pastor or church board that bucked him for taking Timothy away with him; all involved respected this apostle and his ministry. Now, look at the results over time: the fruit of a matured Timothy and his eventual ministry. This strongly affected numerous churches, where Timothy as Titus set eldership in order (Titus 1:5).

Likewise, we see the ministry of the prophet Agabus: "*And as we tarried there many days, there came down from Judaea a certain prophet, named Agabus*" (Acts 21:10). We note that Agabus, as a prophet, traveled to various churches. Few churches will have stationed prophets unless they are of the intercessory prophet function. Upon seeing Paul, the Holy Spirit moved on Agabus with prophetic revelation: "*And when he was come unto us, he took Paul's girdle, and bound his own hands and feet, and said, Thus says the Holy Ghost, So shall the Jews at Jerusalem bind the man that owns this girdle, and shall deliver him into the hands of the Gentiles*" (Acts 21:11). I believe Paul received this Word because he sensed a Holy Spirit witnessing within him. Paul's spirit received assurance that this was from the Lord.

As an apostle and not a prophet, from time to time I receive prophetic insights. The strength that the Lord does give me in revelation matters is that usually I will receive a Holy Ghost witness that comes over my person when a word or Holy-Spirit-given event is spoken of. The anointing witness started as the sensation of goose bumps on my skin. Today, it is mostly by sensing an anointing coming over my mind. The Holy Spirit leads His ministry. I share this detail in order to encourage others to gain understanding of Holy Spirit works.

Think of the treasure given to Paul by these Holy-Spirit-given words. Many will think of the supernatural manifestation that we see in the scripture as Paul's journey unfolds. Now, consider how this affected Paul. By this foretelling, the Lord graciously allowed Paul to ponder these words with expectation, and to prepare for the future, strengthening for when this difficult passage in his life came to pass. The value of strengthening by prophetic gifting is huge. This is a Holy-Ghost ministry that many are denied of—a huge loss to the church.

We see this same ministry effect demonstrated by other prophets: "*And Judas and Silas, being prophets also themselves, exhorted the brethren with many words, and confirmed them*" (Acts 15:32). This confirmation was by prophetic impartation of Holy-Spirit-given insight and knowledge; it spoke to their privately held thoughts. The prophets' ministry brought assurance to strengthen them in their direction, assurance to being correct in what they believed the Holy Spirit was directing them to do in their God walk. Other times, it was by giving prophetic foreknowledge, which would strengthen their resolve many years later.

As a young and zealous ministry member, I held my only tent crusade in Valemont, a mountain town in northern British Columbia, Canada. Mr. King, a mature prophet, attended. I had never met him, yet he spoke to me of a future dealing in my life. I had no understanding of this speaking, as it involved the term "apostle." Some thirty years later, the Holy Spirit reminded me of that word. Thank God! This greatly strengthened my resolve and stability when questions arose from the bends and turns in my life's journey as all experience.

A Plural Elder Ministry Reality

Repeated and needed insight: the first truth is to discern and accept that not all elders are of the five ascension gift callings. The truth of *"if any man desires to be an elder"* is an essential truth to be recognized and understood (1 Tim. 3:1). The Holy Ghost moves within people by impartation of a holy desire (Acts 20:28). All elders need to be encouraged and released to express their ministry. *"It is God Who works within you, to will and do His desire"* (Phil. 2:13).

Demonstrating the great need for the plural eldership is an easy task. This topic is close to any genuine apostle's heart. After having warm relationships with people who were fellow members of a church where I functioned in the pastor's office, I still receive questions and communications from some of them. This is regardless of the fact that I have not been there for some twenty-nine years, and that I now live in a different country.

This is regardless of where they now attend, in churches that believe in "Holy Spirit baptism with tongues and prophecy." Some attend good churches that claim to believe in and uphold the fivefold ministry. When they ask me questions of propriety in their church dealings, I always ask them if they have discussed this with their church elders. The answer is usually no. I always tell them to gently discuss the matter with their leadership. This non-overseeing elder relational gap is painful to observe. Although they may respect the "pastor," the painful truth becomes clear.

They have a dysfunctional, non-fivefold eldership. After attending these churches for a number of years, they have not had any personal home visitations by elders. They have not formed an in-depth relationship with the leaders.

This is sure evidence of failure in the church due to the senior ministry being a pastor. He is limited in real fivefold truths and understanding. While visiting, this leader took no interest in my person after briefly being introduced. He questioned my ministry involvements. I respectfully answered him, then I gave him a fivefold multiple ministry book I had written. Then I did not hear from him. They do not understand or want what a multiple fivefold ministry should be. My person and book threatened the sole authority he strongly guards.

These saints have a home worship group that is known to the church, but they have never had the eldership visit, nor have they demonstrated a concern to encourage their ministry.

All believers should have some close eldership relationships within their church. I am talking about elders who know their people intimately; these individuals should know how the Holy Spirit is dealing in their lives. Encourage them in ministry. This relationship must have a caring responsibility with accountability! Know what their faith challenges are. Know if they are drifting away or if they have a bond with their church family. They need to be embraced with a prayerful, caring Christ focused ministry family. This overseeing care will greatly strengthen the believing church family; it takes an elder's care!

The onefold elder, pastor, prophet, or apostle ministry cannot accomplish this; however, a mature multiple eldership can! (Acts 20:28) We need to discern the called and Christ-appointed elders who are brought to this position by the Holy Ghost. When believers are brought into a fellowship where a onefold "pastor" reigns, the elder care is greatly limited. The believers' maturation and spiritual growth is limited due to the lack of personal care and direction. Apostle headship should bring a change to this; They will focus on multiple elders.

Ask yourself this: am I and the ministry I am involved with part of a scriptural multiple ministry with a genuine apostle's oversight? If not, why not?

CHAPTER SEVENTEEN:
Bold Flock Protection

Expose Wrong Ministry

Protect your people! Guard them from a wrong focus. A fivefold elder-ship must be discerning and bold. Wisdom is always required. Being politically correct is not always God's love or wisdom. One cannot sepa-rate love from truth. When a ministry elder does not understand Christ Jesus' lack of "politically correctness," they miss great truth. Discern the love of God sent to this world when Jesus said, "*Woe unto you, scribes and Pharisees, hypocrites! for ye are like unto whited sepulchers, which indeed appear beautiful outward, but are within full of dead men's bones, and of all uncleanness*" (Matt. 23:27). Jesus labeled Herod as a fox, and Pharisees as snakes and white washed tombs (Luke 13:32, 11:44). Paul, by Holy-Spirit anointing, publicly named people in error: "*Hymenaeus and Alexander; whom I have delivered unto Satan, that they may learn not to blaspheme*" (1 Tim. 1:20).

We MUST protect the flock from wrong teachings by speaking truth in the face of error! True humility is serving Christ by upholding His Word; this will be demonstrated through our preaching and focus. Political cor-rectness must be avoided. Do not be silent in the face of wrong, imbal-anced doctrine. We become servants of men when we are silent. Protect those we are responsible for. Warn our flock when we discern error. Speak out against the wrong information they hear on TV. God holds elders responsible for their actions and inactions: "*My brothers, do not be many teachers, knowing that we shall receive the greater condemnation*" (James 3:1). Jesus tells His disciples, "*The world cannot hate you; but me it hates, because I testify of it, that the works thereof are evil . . . If the world hates you, ye know that it hated me before it hated you"* (John 7:7, 15:18).

Preacher Joel example: Expose wrong teachings! Paul did (see 1 Tim. 1:20; 2 Tim. 4:14). John did (see 3 John 1:9). Our Savior did (see Matt. 23:29). Consider one of today's mega-millionaires, Joel, who is a ministry leader. As a warning to refute and protect our flock from wrong, let us observe this painful example. Joel is a current ministry I intercede and pray for. May he become a minister of life instead of death, as he has a huge following of many thousands with a TV ministry. He authors books, and has a gathering of over sixteen thousand followers on Sundays.

To understand Joel's error, we must see how he applies selective scriptural usage. He ignores the fact that *"all Scripture is God-breathed, and is profitable for doctrine, for reproof, for correction, for instruction in righteousness"* (2 Tim. 3:16). Many people, like Joel, avoid what Paul the Apostle said we are to see: *"Behold therefore the goodness and severity of God: on them which fell, severity; but toward thee, goodness, if thou continue in his goodness: otherwise thou also shalt be cut off"* (Rom. 11:22).

We must understand the balance of truth. There is both goodness [mercy and love] and severity [judgment of moral wrong] in God. Preaching the reality of both truths is of extreme importance. Many people, like Joel, will focus on the goodness and avoid any severity of God's truths. In contrast, we also have a few imbalanced *"severity-of-God"* preachers who forget God's goodness and grace by only preaching damnation and hell. There is a heaven of mercy and love. There is a hell of torment, as well. Either presentation of God, whether it's His goodness or severity, when not balanced with both truths, is an imbalanced untruth.

When preachers like Joel focus too strongly on an imbalanced gospel of goodness, they become vulnerable to being more gracious than God; this happens when they avoid the judgment and severity truths. This is a dangerous road, and it must be avoided.

First point: Joel's error is proven by his teaching in Oprah Winfrey's school, knowing Oprah preaches New Age beliefs. Joel ignores God's separation truth to *"come out from among them."* (2 Co. 6:17). Oprah teaches that a personal relationship with Jesus Christ is not the only way to heaven. In his television interview with Oprah, Joel states his acceptance of this opinion. God's Word by Jesus is, "*He that believeth on the Son hath everlasting life: and he that believeth not the Son shall not see life; but the wrath of God abides on him*" (John 3:36). Oprah preaches that there are more ways to God than one, a universalist belief, but "*Jesus said unto him, I am the way, the truth, and the life: no man cometh unto the Father, but by me*" (John 14:6).

Joel receives and applauds Oprah Winfrey when she visits his church with a celebrity's welcome in his Sunday gathering. I have personally watched a video of this; currently, there is a lot of footage on YouTube that we can all study. Godly preachers will love Oprah enough to tell her of her coming judgment before Christ. They will tell her of hell and her need to repent from her wrong beliefs. They will tell her that Christ and the cross is the only way.

Mr. Joel agrees with Oprah Winfrey that practicing homosexuals will be in heaven. Speaking to Pierce Morgan in a 2014 CNN interview, when asked if homosexuals will be welcomed to heaven, Joel said that they will, and he will not judge this as God will. Joel disregards the following: "*For what have I to do to judge them also that are without? Do not ye judge them that are within?*" (1 Cor. 5:12) Warn your people.

When Pierce Morgan asked Joel and his wife if they would honor a gay friend by attending their wedding, he said, "Of course." Pierce asked how he would treat Elton John, a widely known homosexual who tells people that Jesus Christ was a homosexual. Joel says he would welcome Elton with dignity, as he looks to love people and "not [judge] how they are involved with sin."

Heretic Joel—if he's called of God, and more than just a motivational speaker—should know that his first responsibility is to preach repentance from sin!

God's Word states those practicing homosexual sin will be rejected by Christ: "*Do you not know that the unrighteous shall not inherit the kingdom of God? Do not be deceived; neither fornicators, nor idolaters, nor adulterers, nor abusers, nor homosexuals*" (1 Cor. 6:9). Also, "*if a man also lie with mankind, as he lies with a woman, both of them have committed an abomination: they shall surely be put to death; their blood shall be upon them"* (Lev. 20:13).

God will judge preachers such as Joel, just as He will judge all of us at the end! God judged Sodom and sodomy. Godly preachers will not be shy about God's Word. They will expound: *"Whosoever therefore shall be ashamed of me and of my words in this adulterous and sinful generation; of him also shall the Son of man be ashamed"* (Mark 8:38).

Getting along with everybody has limitations. Read Psalm 1:1: *"Blessed is the man that walks not in the counsel of the ungodly, nor stands in the way of sinners, nor sits in the seat of the scornful."* A godly church will fight against wrong doctrines. They know preachers can depart from the faith they preached and held dear. Apostle Paul, in the Holy Bible, wrote: *"Now the Spirit speaks expressly, that in the latter times some shall depart from the faith, giving heed to seducing spirits, and doctrines of devils"* (1 Tim. 4:1). To *"depart from the faith"* refers to *"the faith"* they once had and now no longer possess (Mark 4:15; 1 Pet. 5:8).

John MacArthur, a strong evangelical preacher, correctly states "Joel never speaks about holiness, humility, fear of God, brokenness, or sacrificial love. He constantly speaks of prosperity and a blessed natural life." We must warn those we are responsible for; warn our people of those who preach with an appeal to the flesh while ignoring *"Follow peace with all men, and holiness, without which no man shall see the Lord"* (Heb. 12:14).

Politically correct ministries will not preserve the church and flock from such misguidedness. Some will disagree to this writing. Some reading this will say, "You are being overly judgmental and ungodly with such statements." Oh, really? I believe that those who ignore the Bible's truths are religious bigots and ungodly. When some are not knowledgeable, that is different. Then again, why are they not scripturally knowledgeable?

Joel knows the scriptures about practicing homosexuals and their judgment, having had these scriptures pointed out by many. He willfully chooses to ignore them, and he misleads his followers. This is a willful rejection and deletion of the Word of God! I personally believe in being gracious and forgiving while restoring the errant. I also apply this scripture: "*A man that is a heretic after the first and second admonition reject*" (Titus 3:10). Joel is a heretic.

This is not simply having bad doctrine; Christ's Holy Word is serious. Genuine godly ministries and believers will not shirk from strong statements spoken by our Savior. They bow to Christ's Word when He says, "*And if anyone takes away from the Words of the Book of this prophecy, God will take away his part out of the Book of Life, and out of the holy city, and from the things which have been written in this Book*" (Rev. 22:19). Do not fear preachers who defile the Word.

The priority in gospel matters is not the seeking of earthly blessings with personal prosperity. Serving Christ with a servant's heart, to minister in His stead and save souls from hell and judgment, must be of a greater priority focus than prosperity. Our Lord taught the correct priority order in life's prosperity matters: "*But seek ye first the kingdom of God, and his righteousness; and all these things shall be added unto you*" (Matt. 6:33). Observe "*first.*"

Understand Christ's statement of, "*And he that takes not his cross, and follow after me, is not worthy of me. He that finds his life shall lose it: and he that loses his life for my sake shall find it*" (Matt. 10:38–39). Joel preaches, "find your blessed life on earth. Be a better you."

Godly preachers preach the cross with an eternal view. Paul, with worship, said, "*I am crucified with Christ: nevertheless I live; yet not I, but Christ lives in me: and the life which I now live in the flesh I live by the faith of the Son of God, who loved me, and gave himself for me*" (Gal. 2:20). This textual truth is radically different from what Joel projects.

Our loving heavenly Father does bring promised blessings to the Christ-loving faithful; these people do attend a Christ-serving life. Regardless, blessings and prosperity must never overshadow the taking up of our cross in our life's focus. I have personally heard Joel respond to questions on a televised program where the orator asked him about the judgment of people and sin. Joel completely avoided confronting sin. He said, "God will do that." No! All preachers who are Christ's servants must and will confront sin. Jesus Christ preached, "repent."

Paul's Gospel

The apostle Paul did not preach "sugar rights." His gospel preaching included salt: the needed reality of the coming judgment: "*And as he reasoned of righteousness, temperance, and judgment to come, Felix trembled*" (Acts 24:25). Righteousness, temperance, and holiness are core truths of the gospel. Those who avoid these topics are wrongly focussed. Unless Joel (and those like him) repent, they will be among those Christ Jesus speaks of:

> "*Not everyone who says to Me, Lord! Lord! shall enter the kingdom of Heaven, but he who does the will of My Father in Heaven. Many will say to Me in that day, Lord! Lord! Did we not prophesy in Your name, and through Your name throw out demons, and through Your name do many wonderful works? And then I will say to them I never knew you*". (Matt. 7:21–23)

These preachers need to study what God said by the prophet Ezekiel, "*But when the righteous turns away from his righteousness, and commits iniquity, and does according to all the abominations that the wicked man does, shall he live? All his righteousness that he hath done shall not be mentioned: in his trespass that he hath trespassed, and in his sin that he hath sinned, in them shall he die*". (Ezek. 18:24) Ministry, wake up! God is the same yesterday and tomorrow. Be bold! Confront political correctness. That is a loveless silencing of truth.

Overcoming Saints

The gospel ends with overcoming believers being saved from an eternal hell in the coming judgment. Our Lord tells all believers that they must "overcome" in all of the seven letters to the churches. Why are there not more messages preached about this needed overcoming? When preachers avoid and delete sin, hell, and the coming judgment from their preaching, then it is good to warn our flock to avoid these. Preach the need to overcome, just as Christ warns the churches: "*To him that overcomes will I give to eat of the tree of life, . . . not be hurt of the second death, . . . they shall be clothed in white*" (Rev. 2:7, 11, 17, 3:5).

We must maintain a balanced focus of salvation truths. This involves our battle within and our walking after the Spirit. This will result in a holy new creature. This new creation has a Christ-focused life. Our worship is in response to salvation from sin, eternal hell, and not being separated from the love of God. Teach our people, "*I beseech you, brethren, mark them which cause divisions and offences contrary to the doctrine which ye have learned; and avoid them*" (Rom. 16:17; Gal. 1:7–9). When we cannot, and have not, taught this scripture (to avoid some), it is due to the fear of man while disregarding a fear of God.

No doubt there are some sincere "born-of-the-Spirit" believers following preachers like Joel. They struggle like an insect that has landed in the spider's web. Should they not free themselves, in time the spider will consume them. We are to be used of our Lord to keep our flock from this danger; this will only be by teaching knowledge and doctrine.

Teach truth: Paul taught, "*come out from among them, and be ye separate, says the Lord, and touch not the unclean thing; and I will receive you*" (2 Cor. 6:17). Paul also taught, "*Be ye not unequally yoked together with unbelievers: for what fellowship hath righteousness with unrighteousness? And what communion hath light with darkness?* (2 Cor. 6:14)

Joel ignores this to their own eternal peril. The excessive grace preachers all preach that a Christian who received the Spirit of God cannot fall away. This teaching negatively affects the thinking and actions of believers; it causes a false security, resulting in Christian lethargy.

This state of lethargic means that we are ignoring the battle we should all be facing, the flesh against the Spirit: "*This I say then, Walk in the Spirit, and ye shall not fulfil the lust of the flesh. For the flesh lusts against the Spirit, and the Spirit against the flesh*" (Gal. 5:16–17; 1 Pet. 2:11). We must be determined to win this interior battle, or we will lose. This is the "overcoming" that Jesus spoke of to not defile our garments of righteousness. This is where Apostle Peter warns us not to be overcome by sin after vomiting up sin (2 Pet. 2:20). Should they take this vomit back, "*the latter end is worse with them than the beginning.*"

True servants of God will teach about the prophet Balaam; He heard God's voice. He was a prophet. Yet, he was a lost soul awaiting his damnation judgment: "*Which have forsaken the right way, and are gone astray, following the way of Balaam the son of Bosor, who loved the wages of unrighteousness*" (2 Pet. 2:15). This man was a prophet. He was on the right way and forsook the right way. This also applies to those who endlessly preach about giving money: "*And through covetousness shall they with feigned words make merchandise of you: whose judgment now of a long time lingers not, and their damnation slumbers not*" (2 Pet. 2:3). (See the author's manual, "Salvation Gained and Maintained," for more information.)

CHAPTER EIGHTEEN:
Problems Disrupting Building

Key Building Hindrances

The first key factor that limits unified fivefold church building is the mini-god of "I"—a focus on "my image" and "my kingdom." To examine this topic, to the best of my knowledge, I will share some needed maturity understandings and failures in my building efforts.

My experiences will be different from yours; however, similarities will always be there. A number of years ago, while struggling with building a local multiple eldership ministry church, a wise apostle advised me to start with brand new Christians. Unfortunately, time has proven that he was mostly correct. My efforts in North America have been dismal compared to overseas. The difference is humility in some of the ministry I deal with over there.

We must determine to nullify and put to death to a self-image focus, how others see us. Do not compare yourself to others. Focus on Jesus. When we focus on how Jesus sees us as we live and minister, good things will happen. Consider God's words to Abraham: *"walk before ME and be thou perfect"* (Gen. 17:1). Quit looking to man!

Due to having an apostle's heart, I would constantly see potential in genuine Christ-appointed ministries. My heart's mission is to encourage while building a multiple eldership ministry team. I naively welcomed all people with open arms. Hindsight learning has brought change in me to this. Avoid my mistakes.

With a giving heart, I would financially give and work overtime to include these free-floating and disjointed ministries to form a collegial team ministry. I will share my failures with the intent of helping others to gain traction and avoid painful errors in these endeavors. We can all learn and avoid failure by listening to those who have "been there." We need each other. We never stop learning.

Looking back, after moving to a new location, my wife and I attempted to humbly reinforce the ministry of others. We desired to serve with humility, to demonstrate a servant's heart. After several attempts to be accepted and join in with ministry to others, I soon learned that being a supportive member is easy; being given room to minister is another thing. My hope was to join and be part of a ministry team, rather than start another church, as several full gospel churches already existed. After two years had gone by, I joined a small full gospel church. We gained the love and trust of the elderly pastor, who was of a small Foursquare church. He appreciated our support of his ministry. We would travel, and this church was a home base of rest. Two years later, he asked us to take over this church. We prayerfully declined and left shortly after. I realized our doing so would not work.

I accepted the truth that one cannot put new wine into old wine skins. Some dear saints we esteemed resisted the change from a pastor headship to a multiple elder ministry structure. We did not want to tear by pushing a multiple eldership church when I discerned this was not wanted. People need to be teachable, or we are wasting our time. Upon our leaving, the pastor gave us a bouquet of verbal flowers. He told the congregation that in his years of ministry, we were the only ones who came to support with respect for his ministry. We never attempted to take over or disrespect his calling and God given placement.

In any called ministry, the internal fires will burn and cause action. We started a home praise and worship group, then doctrinal studies. As well, during all of this, we would be involved with overseas ministry. As this created a group, a couple came along who expressed their desire to be part of building a team with us; our fivefold beliefs quickly made room for them. We made an effort to embrace this "like-minded," unconnected ministry.

A year later, the evidenced reality came home. The woman of the couple wanted her way and control, swaying her "Ahab" husband in the process. When direction was discussed, we made efforts to agreeably oblige, including moving to a new location and more. The wife turned the focus of godly unity, while prayerfully seeking direction. When she could not get her Jezebel's demanded way, she initiated a strong, personal attack on my wife. End of story.

When a ministry couple wants to join in ministry, examine BOTH parts of the couple.

Lesson number one: Go slow to know those who labor among you before committing to their inclusion in common ministry. Test them as guests until after close communication, when their ministry focus is discerned. Do they desire to bond with mutual accountability, for a positive ministry flow?

I believe in women in ministry. It took me some time to learn this when Paul taught *"let your women be silent,"* the Greek word "women (gune)" in rendered *"specifically a wife"* (1 Cor. 14:34). To ask their *"husbands at home"* speaks to maintaining church orderliness, to not disturb a church service, while honoring husband headship in marriage.

While attending a women's Aglow lunch as a local advisor, the invited speaker, being a prophet and a total stranger to me, said, "Sir, you may be pastoring a small church locally, but I want to know you much better. You are a called apostle." We invited him to speak on the following Sunday. After speaking, he handed me a note with four written scriptures. Three of the four were specifically noted in my Bible with the letters "WHS" (witness of the Holy Spirit)—unique scriptures that I experienced a strong anointing to over the years.

Believing in this clearly identified prophet ministry, we encouraged him to join our fivefold building team. Over the next two years, we poured love and finances into this couple. Some things became evident in time. Their focus on ministry travel finances with little or no "elder heart" for the home flock was strongly evidenced. Statements like, "What we need is some more strong tithers" confirmed this. They did not build eldership bridges with the people. We do need to bless traveling ministry. They also need to have an elder's heart demonstrated in the home church. He once spoke on "mutual esteeming," which was encouraging, but preaching truth and living truth are two different matters (Phil. 2:3).

The test: A fortyish woman from a very rough background attended our church. She accepted the Lord in her second church visit. No efforts were made by this ministry couple to welcome or embrace this newly saved person. Instead, they disrupted me from my pastoral focus of wanting to speak to this lady before she left. They were more concerned with trivial matters at the close of the service than speaking to or encouraging this new soul for Christ. The prophet's priority desire was to rush home to watch the football game.

The following week, the prophet was our guest to celebrate a special occasion. We talked over dinner, and I asked what he thought about this new convert. He commented, "Those missing teeth, I would not want to read her mail." The next Sunday, she attended with a glow and was very "cleaned up." With joy, this newly committed to Christ lady testified of an answer to prayer—how a dentist had offered to fix her teeth for free.

After her testimony, and knowing the negative critique he had said, the prophet did not respond with an elder's heart. This weighed heavily on me. How do you build without a heart for the downtrodden and broken? All elders must be hospitable.

As I deeply struggled and prayed into this, I believe the Holy Spirit quickened me to meet and only ask one question. I invited him out for a dessert and coffee break, which he attended, "But only if my wife can come along" (a sign of a problem). During this visit, I posed the question, "Would you be willing to spend some time together to discuss eldership principles with me?" After a couple of his questions were answered, he shook my hand, saying, "I will make time for this before next month." That night, he emailed our people saying a complete untruth: that I had kicked him out of our church. So much for esteeming each other and mutual accountability.

Lesson number one: Go slow to know those who labor among you before committing to the inclusion of other ministry callings. Warmly receive fellow ministry, but be slow to recognize them as fellow elders in the body you are responsible for, before forging a covenant walk with them.

Again, with a heart for the broken in ministry, we accepted and opened our doors to a couple. They had been assistant pastors in a larger local church for many years. He did odd jobs in small construction, contracting, and concrete work. They were broken down and on the verge of losing their home. We received them and remedied the several thousand-dollar financial matter, and then encouraged them in ministry before all. Things seemed to advance fine for a time.

Our business was doing excellent, and this supported us and our travels, besides enabling our giving to the church. We took a long-overdue "timeout" from our extremely busy ministry and business life, which we'd been doing for years. We believed we had some stable church ministry support, and we left for a three-week getaway. Two days before coming home on a Saturday, from a blessed Hawaii sabbatical and a much-needed rest, my dear prophetess wife said, "Honey, you need to brace yourself. The Holy Spirit said that we are about to encounter some severe problems upon coming home." Knowing her, I paid attention. We did.

The Sunday morning service said it all. The following week, we had a discussion with the pastor couple, and they let it be known that they were leaving, and that some people would be joining them. As part of my response, I said, "If that is your choice, do what you believe to be right in your walk. However, let us do this in a mature godly manner." We volunteered to bless them with a $10,000 token of peace and brotherly love, in a unified service the following Sunday, to bless their new direction. Their response said it all: "We cannot do that," thereby verifying their communications and dealings with others.

Without details or discussion, the keys were handed in and most of the church left following them. We do not know all the details, but we do know that we were secretly destroyed to our people. "Sorry, Lord," I am a slow learner.

Lesson number one: (same lesson) Go slow to know them who labor among you before committing to the inclusion of another ministry. The few who stayed are still with us today, and they are strong in doctrine and ministry principles. The pastor couple and another leadership couple, after leaving us, declared personal bankruptcy within a year, as did a young ministry in training who also left. The leader couple who stayed have grown through these events. They are so blessed in all they are doing. This painful memory still grieves my heart.

Lesson number two: In church building, we must learn to be content with those the Lord gives us. Do not fret if this is a small group. Evangelism and growth of the church is wonderful. However, allowing the Lord to build the house is more important. If the body is not taught holy and correct principles, the foundation will not be strong, and it will not be capable of carrying the weight of a genuine fivefold church. God is faithful. Prayerfully follow Him from week to week. He will bless us with His wisdom. Trust God's wisdom. Stay humble, and be teachable. If our focus is to build big without maturing people, we may grow in numbers, but we will fail in what Christ desires from us.

Our focus on maturing our people will become the real road to growth. It is good to desire being effective in reaching many, but the primary focus should be on those who have followed us up the mountain after we have seen the multitude. The scripture of *"trust in the Lord and do not lean on your own understanding"* is so necessary in genuine building (Prov. 3:5). Elijah did not question time spent in his hidden brook experience. He did not know that after this obedience, he would outrun King Ahab's horses; call down fire from heaven, which consumed water and stones, and kill over eight hundred of Jezebel's prophets (1 Kg. 18:38).

The challenge: Our faithful ministry elder couple met what seemed to be a godly ministry couple with musical abilities. They attended services shortly after. This led to involvement with their music and worship abilities. Being more careful now, we spent two evenings with them, thoroughly reviewing our ministry focus, guidelines, and fivefold principles. All of this was received with them saying a loud "amen" to a mutually accountable eldership.

This opened a stronger releasing for the man, as he wanted to teach some things that were on his heart: evangelism and healing the wounded.

In his presentation, he slammed all churches and was insensitive to correction in this regard. Personally, I will strongly confront wrong church doctrine and practices. However, I do thank God for all churches, because they contain the bride of Christ. Some people find salvation in the churches I strongly disagree with (in regards to their doctrine and focus). God knows His servants and their hearts. They are not mine. I thank God for all of them and consider myself to be a "constructive reformer."

Over the next few months, we noticed that the couple never reached out to us in a reciprocal fashion. They made significant efforts and did strongly bond with our faithful, long-term elders. Then the report came in that they had often questioned our elders, asking, "Who is really in charge or in authority here?" Several times, our elders advised them to speak to me; they did not. I prayerfully eliminated them from our church's fellowship. When meeting with them, they did not want to discuss what was involved in bringing this decision about. They responded with an immediate and strongly expressed fury. This only proved the necessity of separating them. The reality was, they wanted our matured elders to come with them, to be part of their vision.

Their questioning of leadership authority matters with our elder couple, while not following the repeated directive to communicate with me, was divisionary.

The lesson: Other callings who want to come in and participate alongside our church must be of an understanding that our vision is an apostle's vision, and not an evangelist's vision when building a church. The apostle's vision embraces all ministries; desiring the fruitful releasing and functioning of all the callings. The evangelist's vision, when it does not embrace the apostle's vision, will solely aim at winning souls and healing the wounded. That vision in itself is good, but to build with a Biblical, apostle-led vision, people need to embrace the truth, which is that all five callings have a vision. All five callings must express their ministry vision with a corporate apostle's oversight. The evangelist and all other callings need to see the importance of the apostle, prophet, and teacher, all with their Holy-Spirit-imparted visions and strengths that the church needs. Winning souls is just part of the picture. To not acknowledge Christ when He says that we need all of these callings, and in a priority order, is wrong.

Lesson number one: (same lesson) Know those who labor among you. In a correct, apostle-led, multiple eldership ministry, before embracing other callings, test new ministry as to their team vision first. This means spending a lengthy amount of personal time testing the waters, discussing unified visions and ministry principles. Do they embrace the total ministry vision as greater than their singular vision? As wild horses, many want to run with the wind without bowing to Christ and His fivefold giving. They want their headstrong personal ministry with no yielding to the team. They say "yes," but they deny acknowledging that all five callings are needed, instead of solely focusing on their one-fold ministry.

Overcoming Problems that Limit Building

Achieving a fivefold ministry is Christ-given, and it is His desire. The failure to do this lies with us. Here are some key building hindrances:

a) **Only seeing my ministry burden and influence as the greatest need and importance:** We must see the Holy Spirit's burden and vision associated with our holy calling as important. Being called to represent the living God and Savior as His ambassador in ministry is of huge importance and responsibility. We must be faithful to minister the Holy Ghost's burden—that is what He wired us for.

   However, we must also look to Christ and His Lordship. We must look for and discern the other four ministry callings. All have been given a sovereign burden. We must attain the maturity of esteeming the burdens and callings of our fellow Christ-given ministry: "*he gave some, apostles; and some, prophets; and some, evangelists; and some, pastors and teachers*" (Eph. 4:11). We must see all of them as needed and important, just as our Lord does.

b) **With self-sufficiency, being blind to equally given fellow ministry callings and their value:** We will not see the need for all callings unless we stop and examine the wisdom and importance of our fellow ministry members and their strengths; the Lord Jesus Christ gave these as a needed ministry. Recognize their focus and burden. Consider the result of the evangelist's fruit without the maturing of the elder, pastor, and teacher. All believers should have elders in the Lord over them (Heb. 13:7). Mature ministries see the negative fruit of churchless wandering souls. Consider the loss of the apostle's governmental insight, which provides a clean-Word doctrinal focus to establish world outreach. Calculate the loss of prophetic revelation to believers, who are never touched by the prophet. We must grow to genuinely esteem our fellow callings (Phil. 2:3). Without a fivefold ministry and scriptural focus, so much is lost due to our disobedience—due to our self-sufficiency, our being blind to equally given fellow ministry callings and their value. This is a horrible form of PRIDE.

Due to the nature of God's call to ministry, there should be a common elder's heart in overseeing—a caring component from all healthy ministry elders. Again, the danger is the big "I"—the temptation is to have the mindset of "I can do it all, and better than others." This onefold mindset is prideful and dangerous. It brings damage to the starving flock who need what the other callings will provide. A onefold mindset kills fivefold church building. Yes, younger ministry members may project simple things for our thinking, but maybe that is what is needed. A teacher will minister with a depth of knowledge, but they have a limited heart for evangelism, and a limited focus towards the prophetic. The church needs all members of the Christ-given ministry orchestra.

c) **Immaturity in not discussing doctrinal matters in order to achieve a unity of mind:** Not discussing doctrinal matters demonstrates our immaturity. Love and patience is needed.

This is an essential topic to be dealt with. To question our need for doctrinal unity while building a multiple fivefold eldership ministry is not valid. Scriptures tell us, "*Now I beseech you, brethren, by the name of our Lord Jesus Christ, that ye all speak the same thing, and that there be no divisions among you; but that ye be perfectly joined together in the same mind and in the same judgment*" (1 Cor. 1:10). With humility, we must prioritize time to attain this.

Disregarding this truth under the guise of love and patience is an act of disobedience to Christ and His Word. For a successful fivefold ministry network to be built, we must strive to *"be perfectly joined together in the same mind and in the same judgment."* The only way to deal with our differences requires loving, mature Bible textual dialogue. This takes real maturity.

d) **Prideful inability to mutually submit to one another:** When we are in a place of authority, the mini-god of "I" arises and tempts us. The saying that "power corrupts and absolute power absolutely corrupts" comes out in ministry, as well as in worldly matters. To not demonstrate what our Lord taught by washing the eleven apostle's feet is a huge barrier to collegial ministry. We note that this was the second-to last lesson before His graduation.

Godly humility and maturity are required to give our Lord the throne in our ministry. Failure to discern and encourage fellow ministry elders disrupts our church building. Look for the value of what their burden strengths provide. They may not be the same as you in their burden, but they will have something that you do not have. We must attain unto a corporate Christ vision. This is what it takes to make Him Lord of our lives and churches.

e) **Looking only to my finances with a protective, territorial outlook:** We cannot build a multiple ministry church when all look for a salary from the church. Church and ministry finances are large topics that need to be scripturally sought out. For a ministry to receive financial support is scriptural. When this support does not consider the needs of all Christ-given ministries, this becomes a barrier to establish what should be. We must study servanthood and attempt to follow all scriptural and spiritual principles in these dealings in order to enable all callings.

To only look to my finances with a protective, territorial outlook—without coming to terms with the financial needs of others—will limit unity in building. Church and ministry finances can greatly increase with the appropriate teaching. We need to examine the scriptures that many ignore. It is godly and not spiritual immaturity for elders to work while ministering. Consider the following scriptures:

1. *"Look not every man on his own things, but every man also on the things of others"* (Phil. 2:4). The "root of all evil" applies to the world and church. When our financial outlook is for a onefold ministry, fivefold ministry will be limited. It will require real soul-searching and effort to make this possible. Look to the realistic needs (and not wants) of others.

2. *"Even so hath the Lord ordained that they which preach the gospel should live of the gospel; But I have used none [NONE] of these things: neither have I written these things, that it should be so done unto me"* (1 Cor. 9:14–15). After spending time setting out detailed rights to help ministry members live by the blessings of the gospel, Paul says, *"I personally do not use this right."* Servanthood ministry was exemplified by Paul in all churches. It takes wisdom and servant heartedness to not limit fivefold ministry due to financial limitations. The banquet table and the flock are precious.

3. Paul lived and taught the following truth to the Ephesus church elders: *"I have coveted no man's silver, or gold, or apparel. Yea, ye yourselves know, that these hands have ministered unto my necessities, and to them that were with me. I have shewed you all things, how that so laboring ye ought to support the weak, and to remember the words of the Lord Jesus, how he said, It is more blessed to give than to receive"* This was addressed to the ELDERS of Ephesus (Acts 20:33–35). This included all ministry callings. Why is this teaching usually skipped over and rarely focused on as a sermon topic? This statement was an exhortation to the ministry, the governing elders of the church of Ephesus. They were admonished to feed, oversee, and bless by giving to the flock through their laboring.

   NOTE: All ministries Paul walked with and raised up, did not place heavy financial burdens on those they ministered to, "Co 12:16 "But be it so, I did not burden you: nevertheless, being crafty, I caught you with guile. 17 Did I make a gain of you by any of them whom I sent unto you? 18 I desired Titus, and with him I sent a brother. Did Titus make a gain of you? walked we not in the same spirit? walked we not in the same steps" (2 Co. 12:16)?

Losing the potential of being a salaried employee paid by God's people will limit many from seeking a genuine fivefold church. Sad but; the truth of servanthood in finances challenges their income security. Carefully with wisdom seek how to overcome this obstacle to promote a collegial ministry church presence. May take some time. The Lord will guide and supply.

4. "*After these things Paul departed from Athens, and came to Corinth; And found a certain Jew named Aquila, born in Pontus, lately come from Italy, with his wife Priscilla; . . . and came unto them. And because he was of the same craft, he abode with them, and wrought: for by their occupation they were tentmakers. And he reasoned in the synagogue every Sabbath, and persuaded the Jews and the Greeks*" (Acts 18:1–4). While preaching and teaching from house to house, and on Sabbath days, Paul planned to act in a secular occupation in order to gain income. Paul also ministered from house to house as he wrote fourteen Bible Books of the New Testament.

5. Paul said; "*And I will very gladly spend and be spent for you; though the more abundantly I love you, the less I be loved. But be it so, I did not burden you: nevertheless, being crafty, I caught you with guile. Did I make a gain of you by any of them whom I sent unto you? I desired Titus, and with him I sent a brother. Did Titus make a gain of you? Walked we not in the same spirit? Walked we not in the same steps?*" (2 Cor. 12:15–18) All ministries whom Paul associated with and those whom he encouraged created their own income. They functioned in building genuine fivefold churches. This may be complicated in today's world, but it is possible with the Lord's help. These are Bible scriptures, and not man's words. Our ministry focus may be wrong when we are "too busy" in ministry. Examine your time usage. Are we sharing ministry work with our fellow elders? Or are they just dealing with the perfection of worshipping, ushering, and practical matters?

6. God' Word; "*Beloved, you do faithfully whatsoever thou do to the brethren, and to strangers; Which have borne witness of thy charity before the church: whom if thou bring forward on their journey after a godly sort, thou shalt do well*" (3 John 1:5–6). When traveling and planting other churches, numerous scriptures demonstrate the expectation

that established churches supplied ministry travel funds, as well as support for church planting.

7. Regretfully, this scripture applies to many popular ministries: *"through covetousness shall they with feigned words make merchandise of you: whose judgment now of a long time lingers not, and their damnation slumbers not"* (2 Pet. 2:3). Personally, I have written to several people who give manipulative scriptural statements in order to gain finances for their livelihood. A common thread is, "send me a one-thousand-dollar faith seed, and the Lord will give you a one-hundred-fold blessing." I have personally warned such people of their pending Christ judgment. My hands are washed from their blood (Acts 20:26; Ezek. 3:18).

8. Honoring the brethren is a holy commandment: *"Be kindly affectionate one to another with brotherly love; in honor preferring one another"* (Rom. 12:10). This honor is not only for elders, but for the marketplace brethren, as well—those who fund ministry as the Lord blesses their business income. They prayerfully pursue financial gain with a godly work and business practice. We tend to honor elders and ministry, but we do not have the same esteeming of those who minister by giving and supporting the ministry. Let them know their marketplace giving is a Christ-honoring ministry. Their business ministry enables fivefold.

9. Emotionally manipulating people to give is wrong. Conversely, it is right and correct to speak of the needs of the ministry. When presenting a need, let the Holy Spirit touch the hearts of the believers. Never manipulate; the gospel damage caused by this is huge. I am not bragging, but rather stating a personal testimony. As a young pastoral ministry, I saw the undue pressure placed on young Christians through financial manipulation. This brought damage to the believers. Zealous ministries continuously pressed for the finances to meet their vision and the church budget needs. Due to this I deeply studied all scriptural truths regarding this topic.

While studying New Testament financial dealings, I saw what Paul did and taught. In response, I made a covenant with the Lord to follow in

Paul's footsteps. (sharing not bragging) This was not always easy, but the Lord greatly blessed my small, residential business as a house-framing contractor. In time, this business grew to custom home building and subdivision and land development. The Lord always supplied.

When traveling overseas, I started with my own financing, with little help. Later, I received more help from those the Lord raised up for traveling ministry funds. This enabled me to participate in church planting, miracle salvation crusades, and doctrinal teachings in conferences. The Lord blessed and supplied. I have never taken a church salary, but I help fellow ministry. Now, being retired with no business income, and being fully busy with ministry duties, I am more frugal with my finances. However, I praise God for His faithfulness and His awesome supply. We are blessed.

My wife and I personally practice and teach tithing blessings as a trust covenant with God. I will always teach that the believer's practice of giving is a form of worship. We return unto the Lord what He has first provided to us by way of our marketplace endeavors.

I also recommend my brother, Dr. Kevin Orieux, of BC, Canada (see the back of the book for his contact info). He has wonderful teachings and insights on church finances and our giving. Dr. Kevin teaches marketplace leaders and their employees how to be released from the bondage of debt by implementing the disciplined financial stewardship of resources. People need to understand how the priesthood prospered. When the priesthood taught holy principles, the people prospered; then, in turn, they prospered by the people. When they failed to teach and guide the people in godliness, the blessings would fail, and the priesthood would hunger.

CHAPTER NINETEEN:
Fellowship versus Building Together

For Christian fellowship, when we meet with apostate church people, we can and must extend our grace to reach them. When spending time with those who are "Christian", but not born of the Spirit, we have to be gracious in our efforts to lead them to a saving faith. Fellowship without the aim of timely discussion is a fallacy and a waste of time. Grace has limitations (Luke 10:11).

Without unity, we cannot build together. Apostle Paul clarified this with, "*Be ye not unequally yoked together with unbelievers: for what fellowship hath righteousness with unrighteousness? and what communion hath light with darkness?*" (2 Cor. 6:14) This also speaks to doctrinal unity; it exposes the false foundation of what many people press for by a false ecumenism theology.

While growing as an assistant pastor, I followed the advice of a respected senior minister and attended several "ministerial meetings." I quit these meetings when I saw the wrangling and difficulty involved in attempting to work with old denominational ministry. There was no unity of understanding and vision; only the appearances of building together. After the years went by, I then clearly understood: unless a ministry is born of the Spirit, there will never be a unified focus in church building. When striving for unity with born-again believers, we have a greater latitude.

Our unity: The basic unity standard is our believing that one must be born of the Spirit to be part of the family of God. I can create fellowships with the Evangelicals, Pentecostals, and Baptist believers. However, when building together with fellow yoked covenant ministries, much more is required. We must have unity with a greater diligence in our doctrinal beliefs.

There are some doctrinal differences that should not limit building a fivefold church in unity, and some that will. Some of our common beliefs are nonnegotiable. One is believing in the baptism of the Holy Spirit as evidenced by tongues, prophecy, and gifts of the Spirit.

Fivefold Building and Wasted Time

Striving to succeed in fivefold ministry building will require a higher standard of agreement and focus among our people in order to achieve the goal.

Wasted time, distracted focus : My observation is that apostles, as all other ministries, can have a wrong focus. While doing "right," they can pursue efforts that swallow up their lives and time. We can miss fulfilling our calling. They see the need and good of churches and ministries around them, desiring to guide them towards fivefold ministry principles. They may see the good of having them join in unified projects, such as intercessory prayer or a collegial ministry focus.

Seeking this has good, but it may not be right for them to devote much time on it. It may cause their failure in addressing and completion of the primary focus of their calling. We make choices in ministry. For example, do we focus on what God has called us to be, or on time-consuming involvements with others and churches who do not embrace fivefold principles. Those who deny apostle led teachings and authority? Through their denial, they ignore Christ and His church government.

Weigh your focus. Is our priority focus to establish and mature those that the Lord has given us? Or are we building where we have no real authority? (See John 17:6–8; Matt. 5:1–2) Are we building up those we are primarily responsible for; those who are accountable to us? Unless other churches and ministry receive apostle oversight, and being part of an apostle authority fivefold structure, we may be wasting our time. When we are received as an overseeing ministry, then our responsibility changes. One major truth to understand is this: "I am NOT responsible for those who are not accountable to me." Also; I am responsible for those who are. This must be considered as we focus on our time usage. Is my ministry part of establishing Christ's heart desire; the establishing of His Biblical church government?

Rather: Examine if it is wise to limit extending ourselves into churches that give us lip service in regards to our calling. Receiving accolades for blessing and encouraging them may be good and gratifying; however, the question is: do they receive us as fellow elders with mutual esteeming, including our authority as Holy-given? If so, they will receive our fivefold focus in government, doctrine, and shared eldership as we build.

Consider focusing on those we oversee who will also receive and follow our teachings, doctrinal training, and the establishing of a multiple eldership government. The followers who climbed the mountain will function in a mutually submissive ministry role. They will welcome and receive our vision. To test your correct focus in time usage, ask yourself this: As I extend myself to others to bless and encourage them, have I fully applied myself to implementing ministry by my eldership and people? Are my people maturing? Our primary responsibility lies in the people who receive our eldership. Ignoring this responsibility may limit the fulfilling of our Christ-appointed ministry.

Accepting invitations and encouraging others toward fivefold New-Testament truths is good; but only when they receive us in our calling. Will those we reach out to, receive us in a ministry leadership role and accept us as more than guests? Building up those who follow us up the mountain is a better time usage than focusing on those who deny Christ's government.

Let others observe our establishing efforts through what we produce. When they are teachable, others will follow our model, seeing what we accomplish. When they approve what we represent, they will seek out our leadership, teachings, and a God-placed shared authority.

An apostle's vision is larger than a city's vision. To achieve the fulfillment of this vision, we must focus, mature, and raise up a mature ministering believer assembly.

When others appreciate and honor apostles, but do not recognize their governmental authority, they are still pridefully rejecting the Christ-given first placement in governmental authority; this applies to prophets (second place) and teachers (third place), as well. Full acceptance of the Christ-given five-ministry callings is a must. We must strive to understand and implement the governmental authority order as it is set out in the Bible. Now, build up Christ given, home-church people. This is our primary responsibility.

All ministries struggle with not seeing greater signs and wonders. The matured Paul experienced these: "*Through mighty signs and wonders, by the power of the Spirit of God; so that from Jerusalem, and round about unto Illyricum, I have fully preached the gospel of Christ. Yea, so have I strived to preach the gospel, not where Christ was named, lest I should build upon another man's foundation*". (Rom. 15:19–20) Seeking Holy Spirit presence will bring an increase in anointing and spiritual gifts. Pray in the spirit (Jude 1:20).

Paul fulfilled his calling in laying foundations and not building on another man's foundations. He focused on what our Lord directed. Especially when building and laying church foundations elsewhere, I rarely do not see healings and miracles. God is faithful.

Having constructed several hundred buildings, I know the value of a good foundation. It is difficult to change a foundation after it is put in place. Laying true foundations in your church and people's lives will fulfill what Christ has called YOU to do and be!

CHAPTER TWENTY:
Grow by Teaching Basic Doctrines

Do Not Be Deceived: Doctrine!

Anyone who attempts to build a genuine fivefold church will limit their success unless they establish their elders first and the body second in the foundational doctrines of our faith. All are limited when people don't understand these doctrines enough to give a minor teaching on them. The first church explosion had certain truth elements involved that created this tremendous growth. One of these truths is, *"And they continued steadfastly in the apostles' doctrine and fellowship"* (Acts 2:42). This was not the church's doctrine, pastor's doctrine, or the teacher's doctrine, but rather the apostle's doctrine. Deeply seek and focus on this.

The apostle Paul told the Hebrew church they were babes because they did not understand the foundational Christian doctrines. Because of this, Paul was limited in teaching deeper truths (Heb. 5:10–14). Apostle Paul then laid out what the apostle's doctrines are:

> *"Therefore leaving the principles of the doctrine of Christ, let us go on unto perfection; not laying again the foundation of repentance from dead works, and of faith toward God, 2 Of the doctrine of baptisms, and of laying on of hands, and of resurrection of the dead, and of eternal judgment".* (Heb. 6:1–2)

When the church ministries and saints do not have these doctrines clearly taught to them, they cannot effectively grow to minister as our Lord desires. God will not permit this! *"And this will we do, if God permit."* (Heb. 6:1, 3). "IF God permit"? Yes, people need to learn the rules of the road before they get behind the steering wheel. Do not talk about a fivefold church if you do not ground your people in foundational doctrines to a level where they can give a clear explanation of them! (See the author's "Fivefold Churches Doctrinal Manual," a forty-two-doctrine truth study.)

Wrong doctrine uprooting (death by a false peace)**:** Jeremiah learned that he could not plant and build unless he first rooted out and destroyed (Jer. 1:10). This "uprooting" involves confronting wrong doctrine. Seeking peace is one Bible truth, but it needs to be balanced with other scriptural truths. We are not servants of man, but of Christ. Many want peace with all and our God does too, through their accepting the cross, Christ and His Lordship. Remember this in ministry. Our Lord Jesus, the love of God to the world, said: *"Think not that I am come to send peace on earth: I came not to send peace, but a sword. For I am come to set a man at variance against his father, and the daughter against her mother, and the daughter in law against her mother in law. And a man's foes shall be they of his own household. He that loves father or mother more than me is not worthy of me: and he that loves son or daughter more than me is not worthy of me".* (Matt. 10:34–37)

Our Savior demonstrated His holy love by confronting the wrongs of religious leaders who taught doctrines of death: *"He answered and said to them, Well has Isaiah prophesied of you hypocrites, as it is written, This people honors Me with their lips, but their heart is far from Me"* (Mark 7:6). Genuine love and truth are inseparable; love confronts to correct. If we love Christ, we will love people enough to confront error and speak truth. What kind of love does not warn those in error? How will we look into the eyes of the condemned who pass by us with their sin-ravaged bodies on that coming judgment day, knowing that we did not tell them? Know this; *"Do ye not know that the saints shall judge the world?"* (1 Cor. 6:2)

Lovingly telling people the truth will preserve many of them from horrible judgment after the second coming. For the unsaved, this event ends with eternal hell! How will we be able to look into Christ's eyes when we were unlovingly silent with a "fear of man"? Christ-loving ministries will pay the price of rejection; our Lord led in this example (Isa. 53:3). They will speak and establish truth with love, for God and for man.

Jesus calls us to be watchmen! Watchmen who do not warn people of the enemy who brings death have blood on their hands. As He states in Ezekiel,

> *"Son of man, I have made thee a watchman unto the house of Israel: therefore hear the word at my mouth, and give them warning from me. When I say unto the wicked, you shall surely die; and you give him not warning, nor speak to warn the wicked from his wicked way, to save his life; the same wicked man shall die in his iniquity; but his blood will I require at thine hand. Yet if thou warn the wicked, and he turn not from his wickedness, nor from his wicked way, he shall die in his iniquity; but thou hast delivered thy soul".* (Ezek. 3:17–19)

It is a cowardly lack of love when we do not warn those who are spiritually dying.

Fivefold Ministry Doctrine: A Needed Change to Rebuild the Church

Great change is needed to rebuild what we name and know to be the church. When we bow to God's Word in our Christian ministry focus, we will again experience a true, restored fivefold church. To restore the government of God with the norms of the fivefold ministry is equal to rebuilding our existing "burned gates"; the burned gates currently hindering the "entering in" of the seeking world.

To achieve this restoration, we need to have sound doctrine while humbly kneeling to God's Word with a servant's attitude. WRONG doctrinal beliefs are the root of the fivefold ministry's destruction, bringing great death by limiting an effective gospel ministry.

To repeat the following truth, due to its gravity: We must live the mandate given to Jeremiah and us: *"Then the LORD put forth his hand, and touched my mouth. And the LORD said unto me, Behold, I have put* *my words in thy mouth. See, I have this day set thee over the nations and over the kingdoms, to root out, and to pull down, and to destroy, and to throw down, to build, and to plant".* (Jer. 1:9–10) This is tough work! Change is desperately needed.

This change requires holy zeal, as well as radical submission to Christ and His Word. It involves departing from and then confronting wrong traditions. It requires the roots of our love for Christ and His church. God's people are limited from entering into the place of worship due to the "burned temple gates"—that is, the ministry government of today. Many believers are malnourished by a onefold, one-course meal instead of the banquet table Christ desires to give His church. Huge numbers never see a demonstration of the Holy Ghost's power. Fivefold ministry government must be restored; this will mature His people and greatly improve how much we can reach this dying world.

Believe the prophesied Word of God, as Peter explained to the masses: *"This is that which was spoken by the prophet Joel; And it shall come to pass in the **last days**, says God, I will pour out of my Spirit upon all flesh: and your sons and your daughters shall prophesy, and your young men shall see visions, and your old men shall dream dreams: And on my servants and on my handmaidens, I will pour out in those days of my Spirit; and they shall prophesy".* (Acts 2:16–18) Those who deny this promise of the *"last days"* frustrate God's Word. This should frustrate the spirit of all godly preachers! Peter quoted this approximately two thousand years ago. Peter cited Joel's prophesied Word to the believing regarding the early rain. Joel also prophesied the coming *"latter rain".* Many years after Pentecost James wrote about our Father, the husbandman; His waiting for the coming fruit of the *"latter rain"* (James 5:7).

Again, when Peter spoke of the promise, he referred to receiving the "gift" of the Holy Ghost; this baptism is referred to as "the gift" in several scriptures (see Acts 8:20, 10:45). For example: *"Then Peter said unto them, Repent, and be baptized every one of you in the name of Jesus Christ for the remission of sins, and ye shall receive **the gift** of the Holy Ghost. For **the promise** is unto you, and to your children, and to all that are afar off, even as many as the Lord our God shall call".* (Acts 2:38–39) Many falsely deny this promise, *"and to your children".* Unbelief says, "This cannot be for us who are the 'called afar off." I get tempted to mail a letter with scissors to those who disbelieve this, asking them to cut out this scripture portion.

Our risen Lord met with his eleven apostles, breathed on them, and said, "*Receive the Holy Ghost*" on the evening of the resurrection day (John 20:22). After this experience, they were directed to wait in Jerusalem for "**the promise** of the Father." After waiting fifty days, they were "baptized in the Holy Ghost," and received the promise: "*behold, I send **the promise** of my Father upon you: but <u>tarry ye in the city of Jerusalem</u>, until ye be endued with power from on high*" (Luke 24:49). This was a baptism that brought power, and not the birth that brought Holy Spirit life. They had already received this on the resurrection day when Christ "breathed on them". This brought "power", the demonstrated gifts of the Spirit for ministry. Neither tongues nor prophecy were evidenced when Jesus "breathed upon them," but these gifts were evidenced at Pentecost when 120 were baptized in the Holy Spirit.

Today, all who seek with faith and expectancy will likewise receive. Blind theologians twist, avoid, and disregard these scriptures. Our Lord Jesus discussed this topic with His disciples after He rose from the dead: "*For John truly baptized with water; but ye shall be baptized with the Holy Ghost not many days hence. . . . But ye shall receive power, after that the Holy Ghost is come upon you: and ye shall be witnesses unto me both in Jerusalem, and in all Judaea, and in Samaria, and unto the uttermost part of the earth*". (Acts 1:5, 8).

The power baptism (not birth) comes to those who already have salvation. This is the result of an experiential spiritual immersion. Spiritual gifts, a prayer language of the Spirit, and prophecy are all experiential. All born-of-the-Spirit believers should seek this baptism until they receive.

The only textual "evidence" that some evangelical Christians use to uphold their unbelief that the baptism with tongues or prophecy was only a first-century experience is this: "*For we know in part, and we prophesy in part. But when that which is perfect is come, then that which is in part shall be done away*" (1 Cor. 13:9–10). They erroneously claim that the Bible is perfect therefore the need for spiritual gifts has been erased. When the "perfect is come", is when we will be are perfected in heaven. Their horrible theology ignores the rest of this writing: "*For now we see through a glass, darkly; but then face to face: now I know in part; but then shall I know even as also I am known"* (1 Cor. 13:12). The "perfect" spoken of here refers to when we see Christ face to face in heaven; only then shall we know as we are known.

CHANGE will come, and it will result from teaching and practicing the impartation of this doctrinal truth: the experiential baptism of the Holy Spirit. This is essential to bringing fivefold churches into a genuine reality. This doctrine affects the ministry of our fellow believers.

As an apostle with the appropriate Holy-Spirit wiring, my burden and vision is to build genuine fivefold churches, honoring Christ for His giving of the five differing callings. We need the Biblical multiple elder-ship working together. Scriptural church ministry government has been torn, along with the Holy-Spirit baptism. We must restore the Bible's truths and the fivefold churches. Seek to restore what the devil has torn: specifically, that which differs from the New Testament's portrayal of the church.

Foundational Church Salvation Doctrines

To discuss the church, all must know the basic true doctrines (Heb. 6:1-2); if they do not, the deeper truths will not be understood. Establishing the fivefold ministry truths will not take place without having the basic foun-dational doctrines strongly taught and clarified. We begin by recognizing that Christ is our Lord! (John 20:28) Every journey has a starting point. My wife Siony always says, "do not skip over the process".

We need a strong understanding of man's state of spiritual death, as well as our salvation in Christ: *"And you hath he quickened, who were dead in trespasses and sins"* (Eph. 2:1). We must also treasure knowing God's works and purposes in salvation. Know that in all of the world's history, He is building His church (Matt. 16:18). Our Father's focus of gathering souls by His love via Christ, our salvation is the sole purpose of our world's existence.

Man's fall and God's judgment: God created man in His image. Man is a moral and knowledgeable being (Gen. 1:26). God set the limits for man—that is, what He allowed man to do: *"But of the tree of the knowledge* *of good and evil, thou shalt not eat of it: for in the day that you eat thereof you shalt surely die"* (Gen. 2:17). Man died spiritually when God the Holy Spirit separated from man when he, by his will, chose to become a god unto himself. Man thereby denied God, his Creator. Due to this act of denial, physical death eventually resulted. Man followed the tempter and partook of the forbidden fruit, accepting the lie of *"you shall not die"* (Gen. 3:4–6).

Then we see God's judgment of man, which was the result of sin. We are told of the difficulty a woman would experience in birthing with a depreciated body. Man would earn food by the sweat of his brow as he labored with the cursed ground (Gen. 3:16–17).

God's father's heart: We immediately see God's father's heart and His salvation plan that came simultaneously with the curse. The curse included these words: *"cursed is the ground <u>for thy sake</u>; in sorrow shalt thou eat of it all the days of thy life"* (Gen. 3:17, KJV). *"For thy sake"* means "for man's benefit." This wording is changed to "because of you" in some poorer translations. Who would seek God if all were perfect in life—if there was no pain with prosperity for all, and no one had negative relationships?

In reading *"for thy sake,"* we see God's grace and Father's heart; we see His desire that all men might be saved. Our Savior taught us to pray the following: *"Our Father, who art in heaven"* (1 Tim. 2:3–4; Matt. 6:9).

God's love and redemption in Christ: The promise of salvation is this: *"of him are ye in Christ Jesus, who of God is made unto us wisdom, and righteousness, and sanctification, and redemption"* (1 Cor. 1:30). Also: *"Neither is there salvation in any other: for there is none other name under heaven given among men, whereby we must be saved"* (Acts 4:12). We are a blood-bought people. Christ died in our stead. Christ was sinless and fulfilled the law of righteousness, which exposes our sin, *"that he might reconcile both unto God in one body by the cross, having slain the enmity thereby"* (Eph. 2:16).

Christ Jesus, our Lord and Creator, took upon Himself the form of man for the sole purpose of doing what man could not do, which is atone for our sin: "*Christ Jesus, Who, being in the form of God, thought it not robbery to be equal with God:* **made himself of no reputation**, *and took upon him the form of a servant, and was made in the likeness of men: . . . and became obedient unto death, even the death of the cross*" (Phil. 2:6–8). That is the love of God! Glory! Hallelujah! Praise Him! Our God is morally Divine! God's judged; the holy died for the unholy.

Truth: Salvation involves two unchanging and nonnegotiable truths. First, all believers must be "born of the Spirit." Those born of the Spirit are His: "*ye are not in the flesh, but in the Spirit, if so be the Spirit of God dwells in you. Now if any man have not the Spirit of Christ, he is none of his*" (Rom. 8:9). Second, all believers must have their name *written* in the Book of Life: "*And whosoever was not found written in the book of life was cast into the lake of fire*" (Rev. 20:15). These two truths must both exist in our lives, or else we are still in a state of spiritual death: "*And you hath he quickened, who were dead in trespasses and sins*" (Eph. 2:1). This "quickening" takes place when we are born of the Spirit and our names are placed in the "Book of Life." This is regardless of age. This takes place after the following has happened: "*In whom ye also trusted, after that ye heard the word of truth, the gospel of your salvation: in whom also after that ye believed, ye were sealed with that Holy Spirit of promise*" (Eph. 1:13). By God's grace, He deems children as holy when one parent is a believer (1 Cor. 7:14). This gives great comfort if a young child should die prematurely (1 Kings 14:12–13). Entered names can also be removed from this book (Rev. 22:19, 3:5; Exod. 32:33; Ps. 69:28).

A genuinely born-of-the-Spirit believer must pursue a godly presence walk and life: "*Wherein in time past ye walked according to the course of this world, according to the prince of the power of the air, the spirit that now works in the children of disobedience*" (Eph. 2:2). This walk and pursuit negates the judgment that awaits those who deny Christ: "*He that believes on the Son hath everlasting life: and he that believes not the Son shall not see life; but the wrath of God abides on him*" (John 3:36). In terms of the world's salvation, this truth applies. No matter what ministry preach, those who seek shall find God. Job, Abraham, and the Ethiopian eunuch all had an idolatrous heritage, but they sought the Lord and found Him.

They did not have scriptures (2 Chr. 16:9) Again: all the seeking shall find (Matt. 7:7).

Doctrine Affecting the World's Salvation

Many more will be saved by more preaching. As it reads in Romans: "*How then shall they call on him in whom they have not believed? and how shall they believe in him of whom they have not heard? and how shall they hear without a preacher? And how shall they preach, except they be sent? As it is written, How beautiful are the feet of them that preach the gospel of peace, and bring glad tidings of good things*". (Rom 10:14–15) We are strengthened in ministry when we see our heavenly Father's unfathomable love and plan, as the apostle Paul said: "*He hath chosen us in him before the foundation of the world, that we should be holy and without blame before him in love*" (Eph. 1:4). Our God is "omniscient".

God foreknew two truths that apply to our salvation. The first is that only a sinless, righteous man could atone for man's sin. Secondly, we see Christ, who by His mercy and grace, took upon Himself the form of man: "*Who, being in the form of God, thought it not robbery to be equal with God: But made himself of no reputation, and took upon him the form of a servant, and was made in the likeness of men: And being found in fashion as a man, he humbled himself, and became obedient unto death, even the death of the cross*". (Phil. 2:6–8) God in Christ, by His love and cross, is our faith anchor.

When we understand that our ministry is the means of reaching people to enter into the completion of God's plan, we gain much. The focus of our ministry and faith vision must be the culmination of His plan: "*And I John saw the holy city, new Jerusalem, coming down from God out of heaven, prepared as a bride adorned for her husband*" (Rev. 21:2). In ministry, we must constantly see life through these truth glasses. Seeing the overwhelming love of God and His purposes. That evokes and maintains our ministry vision and is the anchor of our hope.

The Devil's Lie of a "Once Saved, Always Saved" Doctrine

Regarding doctrine Paul said a key truth, "Now I beseech you, brethren, by the name of our Lord Jesus Christ, that ye all speak the same thing, and that there be no divisions among you; but that ye be perfectly joined together in the same mind and in the same judgment" (1 Co. 1:10). This same mind unity is a must when building a collegial multiple elders fivefold church. Therefore, it behooves us to patiently, and graciously reconcile where we differ.

The doctrine of "once saved, always saved" affects the believer's ministry, what they project in grace and holiness, thereby this affects ministry and fivefold church building, as well. Many who embrace this mistaken belief become lethargic and stop seeking a Holy-Spirit walk and fruit-bearing (Luke 8:7).

This is a strongly debated doctrine that separates churches. It is commonly termed "eternal security," or the "perseverance of the saints" by Calvinistic churches. I strongly believe that the Bible teaches that a born-of-the-Spirit believer can lose their salvation. Those who disagree deny numerous scriptures which speak to this topic. Denial of this doctrinal truth tempts believers into a life of presumptuous sin. We must find and teach our people the five scriptures written by four Bible authors, that speak of having covenant people's names removed from God's Book of Life. This is due to God's clear statement that without holiness, we will not see God. The church is taught to "*follow peace with all men, and holiness, without which no man shall see the Lord*" (Heb. 12:14). "No man", (not some) includes all believers.

While building together with others, should I be silent in regards to my beliefs on this matter? This is a different topic than the questions regarding eschatology—the debate over the exactness of when Christ will come back; that truth does not affect one's salvation. My view and concern in this is not to just be more correct than someone else; this matter affects the believer's life now, as well as their eternal salvation. Believing that one cannot fall from faith and salvation affects Christians in the fruitfulness of their ministries.

The Bible also sets out the great truth that we will not be saved due to our works, but by our faith in what Jesus accomplished for us by the cross. Then again; the apostle James also said *"faith without works is dead"* (Jms. 2:26). Al believers face the choosing of our focus in life, whether for Christ or ourselves. This is a constant daily choice after receiving our salvation. The "brother" who got involved with fornication in 1 Corinthians chapter five, was dealt with by *"bind such a one over to Satan, for the destruction of the flesh, that His spirit MAY* [might] *be saved in the day of the Lord* [rapture] (1 Co. 5:5).

As mentioned above, many who embrace this wrong belief become lethargic which we are warned against, due to "having arrived" with no need to "overcome" They now just wait for heaven. Peter said, *"beware lest ye also, being led away with the error of the wicked, fall from your own steadfastness"* (2 Pet. 3:17).

I see it as my necessary responsibility to preach the following: *"Work out your own salvation with fear and trembling"* (Phil. 2:12). The "once saved always saved" preachers never preach the why of this scripture, why "with fear and trembling". I believe all Christians should know what the Apostle Paul taught when he revealed what he and we believers are all vulnerable to; he wrote, *"when I have preached to others, I MYSELF should be a castaway"* (1 Cor. 9:27). This sounds unusual: Paul, vulnerable to being a "castaway?"

The Greek word for "castaway" means to be eliminated and rejected. This is Bible textual truth! When we ignore our responsibility to *"work out [our] own salvation,"* the Bible states that it is possible that we can become a *"castaway,"* or a rejected people. Some deny these scriptures which I respect!

Responsibility by Our Conscience

Preaching this truth is my ministry responsibility: *"Wherefore I take you to record this day that I am pure from the blood of all men. For I have not shunned to declare unto you all the counsel of God"* (Acts 20:26–27). As a servant and apostle of Christ, I must have the liberty to preach what I believe to be essential doctrine.

I must also preach, *"Wherefore the rather, brethren, give diligence to make your calling and election sure: for if ye do these things, ye shall never fall"* (2 Pet. 1:10). These scriptures are avoided by preachers who believe that one can never fall away—either that, or they will give a torturous rendition by their untextual theology. Not to overly belabor this truth, but being deeply burdened, I warn all who do not understand; we who have received Christ can come to a place the Hebrew church was warned about:

> *"For it is impossible for those who were once enlightened, and have tasted of the heavenly gift, and were made partakers of the Holy Ghost, And have tasted the good word of God, and the powers of the world to come, If they shall fall away, to renew them again unto repentance, seeing they crucify to themselves the Son of God afresh".* (Heb. 6:4–6)

Avoided truth: Most preachers sidestep the words "fall" or fall away," or they give a torturous reasoning that those who *"fall away"* were not really saved. This scripture clarifies this truth. They cannot be renewed to repentance. They once did repent from sin. We are still tempted by sin. They gave into temptation and did not repent, but went back to Egypt and their vomit choosing sin (immorality, etc.). They came to a place where they now "cannot" be brought to repentance again. The blood of Christ shed for their salvation by Jesus' crucifixion was negated. Jesus Christ will not come to be crucified a second time for them. Without the ability to repent, we cannot be saved. Theologians, ask yourself this question, why would God mention the needed potential of Christ having to be crucified a second time? The reality.

For those who are unclear in this doctrinal truth, ask yourself; how did some come to a place where they can no longer repent? This scripture says that they now cannot repent—not "will not." The Holy Spirit will no longer convict them of sin: *"And when he is come, he will reprove the world of sin, and of righteousness, and of judgment"* (John 16:8). Without Holy-Spirit conviction, the result is eternal death. Holy-Spirit grace is described here: "*For godly sorrow works repentance to salvation not to be repented of: but the sorrow of the world works death*" (2 Cor. 7:10; John 16:7). This is why we are told not to grieve the Holy Spirit by presumptuous sin: "*And grieve not the Holy Spirit of God, whereby ye are sealed unto the day of redemption*" (Eph. 4:30). These people have grieved the Holy Spirit. Preach this Bible text and the potential result of this. Godly fear is needful (Phil. 2:12).

After his adultery and murder of Uriah, David pleaded with God not to take the Holy Spirit away from him due to his presumptuous sin (see 2 Sam. 11:15; Ps. 19:13, 51:10–11). Paul wrote, "*For if we sin willfully after that we have received the knowledge of the truth, there remains no more sacrifice for sins*" (Heb. 10:26). Believe this Holy Word! Paul wrote the word "we." WE! This included Paul as the author. We can come to a place where our received blood atonement will no longer apply.

Doctrinal Unity

I do love and appreciate ministries who differ from me. In the big picture I relate to their heart burden and ministry practice. Yet if we were to be in a common building zone, coming to one mind in this regard is imperative. We cannot use a wrench and turn the nuts and bolts in each other's minds. However, what we can do, is reason with the use of scriptures. When there is no heart to reason, there is a prideful, loveless wrong. In time, this will limit our unity as we build.

Regardless, all of us must understand our need for a love walk that will function with a mature grace—a walk that is secondary to essential doctrines. Our priority must also be that we are faithful to God and His Word, while also seeking to be at peace with man. Peter taught believers (not the world) that we are to add to faith: "*beside this, giving all diligence, add to your faith virtue; and to virtue knowledge; and to knowledge temperance; and to temperance patience; and to patience godliness; and to godliness brotherly kindness*" (2 Pet. 1:5-7).

Peter continues with the following admonishment:

> "*Whereby are given unto us exceeding great and precious promises: that by these ye might be partakers of the divine nature,*

> *having escaped* the corruption that is in the world . . . But he that
> lacks these things is blind, and cannot see afar off, and *has forgot-*
> *ten* that he *was purged* from his old sins. 10 Wherefore the rather,
> brethren, give diligence to **make your calling and election sure:**
> for if ye do these things, ye shall never fall". (2 Pet. 1:4, 9–10)

We can forget after we are cleansed from our sin and have "escaped" the corruption in the world by Christ, that we were [past tense] cleansed from our sin. This warning is to us. We have "*escaped the corruption that is in the world*" (2 Pet. 1:3). The line "*forgotten that he was purged from his old sins*" says those who were once were cleansed no longer are. Peter writes this Holy Truth to those who had escaped but are now captives again. They chose to continue to be involved with sin. This, "***has forgot-ten*** *that he **was purged** from his old sins.* " applies.

Preachers should read and teach this , as this is written to brethren. "***Brethren****, give diligence to make your calling and election sure*" (2 Pet. 1:10). This is our responsibility. This is addressed to "*brethren*"—not to the unsaved world. Why are brethren told to make their election sure? That is because they can lose their election, as well as the promises given to the elect. The unsaved world is never referred to as "brethren" or "the elect."

Many preachers only teach that nothing can separate us from the love of God. That is true; no exterior power or being can do this. This truth is written to the faithful "elect"—those who have made their election sure (Rom. 8:29–33). No exterior demon or power exists that can separate us from God's love; only we can. The flesh-against-the-spirit battle within can only be won by us as we seek and lean on Jesus and withstand sin. This truth does not negate other scriptures: "*Submit yourselves therefore to God. Resist the devil, and he will flee from you*" (James 4:7). We never lose our will. We are held responsible for our choices. We can still choose sin to make golden calves and commit adultery as David did. When we continue in these failures, we can come to the place where repentance is no longer available to us.

As we choose to receive Christ in salvation, we must also choose to walk with Him loving and seeking holiness. We, like Judas, can lose our relationship with God. We do not lose our will or our responsibility for same when we get saved. By saying it is not possible to fail, we thereby say we no longer have temptations. , We choose to resist the devil (James 1:12, 4:7). God still holds us responsible for our will and the choices we make. Failure in this doctrine is a disregard of Bible truth warnings.

Peter tells us, the believing church, of our responsibility: *"But he that lacks these things is blind, and cannot see afar off, and hath forgotten that he was purged from his old sins. . . . for if ye do these things, ye shall never fall"* (2 Pet. 1:9-10). He also tells us, *"For if after they have escaped the pollutions of the world through the knowledge of the Lord and Savior Jesus Christ, they are again entangled therein, and overcome, the latter end is worse with them than the beginning"* (2 Pet. 2:20). They had escaped, but got entangled again, and came to a worse end? Our God has expectations of us. Our genuine love walk is proven in and by our desert journey. Do not fail as many have. Become part of the "few" in Sardis who will walk in white.

Many believers do not add to their faith as they should (2 Pet. 1:5). Many receive salvation with joy, then they do little or nothing to not fall away. Many shine for a moment and do not make their "election sure." This is what we are to do, and not what God does for us.

WHY: Why do I focus on this topic when the main topic is how we are to build fivefold churches? It is because **this topic affects our focus, vision, and mindset,** especially as it applies to the ministry of the believer. It affects unity as we build in common. It affects the warnings of danger in what we build. The church is warned not to lose our first love; this can result in our candlestick (light) being removed. The church of Sardis was warned that as they were, only a few of them would walk in white (the robe of righteousness). All were told to overcome. In regards to us, all were warned that our names can be removed from the Book of Life (see Rev. 2:4, 3:4-5; Exod. 32:33). We have been warned. Our faith will be proven by our works until the end. Consider Solomon, who built the magnificent temple. At his life's end, he built a temple across from God's temple for the idol God, Chemosh (1 Kings 11:7).

Church Reformation

"Reformation" refers to those gospel warriors who bring the church back to doctrinal truths that have been lost or destroyed. The completion and end of reformation occurs when churches function and look like what we read about in the Book of Acts. God has one church, not two. It will take a determined holy reformation to bring this "one church" about. It will require correction in doctrinal beliefs as well as our conduct in worship services.

The correction of doctrine is what birthed church reformation in history by past reformers. Likewise, this correction is an ongoing fact in the continuing and needed reformation today. The living versus the apostate church. We must again look like our holy blueprint, as it was given in the New Testament. Fivefold ministry truths will establish this.

Understanding Different Bible Versions

A brief history of Bibles and translations is needed to understand sound doctrine. The Authorized King James Bible was translated by some fifty Hebrew and Greek scholars. This work was commissioned by King James of England, and it was completed in 1611. The translation was from the *Textus Receptus*, the "received Text" manuscript that largely compares to the Roman Catholic Church's *Vaticanus* manuscript, which is held in their possession.

In 1881, revisers of the King James Bible revised this work to the "Revised Version." This revision was undertaken by people who were limited in Greek and Hebrew. They made changes to the English of the King James translation ignoring the Greek and Hebrew in many cases. A classic example of change is found in Hebrews, 6:2; The Bibles used in the denomination I grew up in changed the King James "doctrine of baptisms to "various and sundry teachings of washings and ablutions." Many Bibles contain changes from the original text and King James scholarly translation.

Then along came the major Bible change, resulting in the "American Standard Version" of 1901. This is what later Bible translations were based upon. I highly recommend a small inexpensive book entitled *God Wrote Only One Bible*, available from Eye Opener Publishers. This book thoroughly sets out the 5,337 changes that two Roman Catholic men, Westcott and Hort, made to the Greek *Textus Receptus* and the King James Bible.

Documented letters from Westcott and Hort are as follows. Westcott wrote the following letter from France after leaving a monastery in 1847: "After leaving the monastery we shaped our course to a little oratory which we discovered on the summit of a neighboring hill . . . Fortunately we found the door open. It is very small, with one kneeling place; and behind a screen was a small pieta' the size of life [i.e., Virgin Mary and the dead Christ]. . . . had I been alone, I could have knelt there for hours." [God Wrote Only One Bible, Eye opener Publishers]

Hort writes to Westcott, October, 17th, 1865: "I have been persuaded for many years that Mary-worship and Jesus-worship have very much in common in their causes and the results."

By knowing the source, we see the fallacy of altered translations. One can find salvation by most any Bible, but in doctrinal matters, the basic text is extremely important.

Receiving and Believing Clearly Set Out Text

My frustration level and struggles with those who deny clearly set out textual truths has grown over the years. I see the tremendous damage this does to the believers, churches, and Kingdom of God. Our Savior often confronted this. Dealing with the Pharisee ministry of His day, *"Jesus answered and said unto them, ye do err, not knowing the scriptures, nor the power of God"* (Matt. 22:29). As Jesus, we must confront doctrinal error today. Godly ministry are called to this. Those who deny a personal and experiential baptism of the Holy Spirit need to hear these same words. Those who today deny Christ and His Lordship by denying His giving of the five scriptural ministry callings also need to receive *"it is written."*

How great is our God? How awesome is His mercy towards us? How tremendous is His loving patience towards man? Daily, He pursues and reaches souls throughout the world. The gentle Holy Spirit continually draws men to truth and Christ our Lord. He also responded to the Ananias and Saphira lie (Acts 5:5). Our God is holy!

In His continual pursuit of building His church, our heavenly Lord and God uses us, His saints. Christ uses His army. He guides us with the five callings of the apostle, the prophet, the teacher, the pastor and the evangelist. Soon, when the harvest is ended, time will be no more. We must do our part.

We love you, Lord Jesus, for the cross. We love you, Holy Spirit, for drawing us to the Father. We love you, our heavenly Father, for your unspeakable love beyond description, for salvation's plan. We love you, our Savior and Lord Jesus Christ. You brought salvation down to man and me. Restore your church, oh Lord, with holy power, miracles, and your anointing presence.

SUMMARY

Church ministry truth: The Bible tells us, by Christ's words, that "*when he ascended up on high, he led captivity captive, and gave gifts unto men*" (Eph. 4:8). These gifts are as follows: "*He gave some, apostles; and some, prophets; and some, evangelists; and some, pastors and teachers*" (Eph. 4:11).

The five ministry callings, given to mankind, need to be discerned and allowed to flow in a loving, complimentary ministry. World evangelism and church establishing will greatly multiply when this truth is scripturally embraced and established in all churches.

The first-century church was known as the following: "*These [believers] that have turned the world upside down are come hither also*" (Acts 17:6). The reason why we have not turned our world upside down is because we have disregarded Christ's fivefold giving in our church building. We have denied Christ's appointed authority structure. We have not discerned or embraced the different callings of our fellow called ministry, as Christ would have us do. Our churches are so different from what is portrayed in the New Testament. There is only one church and one body; regardless of whether it is immediately after Pentecost or now, as we are nearing the end of time and looking for the second coming of Christ. This one body should not differ from the initial churches that were planted by the original apostles.

There is no scriptural reason to have a different church from what we read about in the New Testament's Book of Acts. Man has changed the church through unbelief (1 Cor. 12:12).

Many know the scriptural commandment to establish godly churches in the world: "*Therefore go and teach all nations, baptizing them in the name of the Father and of the Son and of the Holy Spirit*" (Matt. 28:19). This commandment was not spoken to the general disciples who followed Him, or to the seventy disciples Jesus had previously sent out. Our Lord separated and set apart the eleven apostles: "*And the eleven disciples went into Galilee, to the mountain where Jesus had appointed them*" (Matt. 28:16).

Jesus Christ specifically gave the "Great Commission" command to His remaining eleven apostles. The church is to be more than what some now term as "apostolic." The apostles were commissioned to implement and oversee the "go into the world" responsibility. Usually, this is avoided while claiming to be "apostolic". We must seek out Christ-given and discerned apostle headship! The church is to be led by genuine and discerned mature apostles!

The Christ-given Great Commission does involve all believers, but it is apostle-led. When the mature and right-spirited apostles are again accepted and given their place, they will lead in this responsibility of ministry, bringing back a church that is equal to the Book of Acts.

Fivefold Fishing: Let us conclude with an example. If a fivefold ministry was compared to fishing and the members' different strengths were used within the same team, it would look something like this.

All of the church and ministry members know that there are fish to be caught in the lake. The apostle would see the need for the boat, net, and team required to catch and process the fish, and they would responsibly seek to acquire these things. The prophet would be listening to the Holy Spirit in order to know the time, location, and depth that would make the team most successful. The teacher would be studying, and he would provide the knowledge about the species and bait types in order to maximize the catching, cleaning, and preserving of the fish so as to not have waste.

The evangelist, with excitement, would get help, go out regardless of time or weather, and be tireless in casting his net to maximize catching all he can possibly gather. The pastor would carefully receive the catch, clean it, and care for the processed fish. All the elders would distribute this catch with wisdom and love, while also ministering to the assembly.

The well-fed believers would then minister both inside and outside of the church.

The successful result of Building a fivefold church, will be observed by a number of changes to the current "status quo":

There would be a welcoming of all of the Christ given gift callings, with doctrinal unity, to be received in the ministry of revelation knowledge, focus of vision and gifts of the Spirit. There would be a different church service format where the attending church body will be encouraged to participate by flowing in Holy Spirit gifts and Word insights. All would be bringing in the results of their ministry; the souls they are ministering to in salvation and maturing of same. This church will recognize an apostle led multiple eldership governmental authority order, as Christ provided per His desired setting in all churches.

The result of fivefold ministry restored truths includes experiencing healings, miracles, demonstrated authority over demons and Holy Spirit manifestations. When the church is as God desires where Jesus Christ is Lord, we will see massive evangelism with a huge harvest. We will experience seeing the fruit of the promised latter rain harvest. We will see the army that Joel speaks of in the Day of the Lord (Joel 2:1-11)! All of this as the soon coming sun refusing to shine; the moon turning to blood and men's hearts failing because of the sea roaring and the waves thereof (Lk. 21:45); as we approach the Day of the Lord Jesus Christ, as He gloriously comes for us, His church. I believe! Praise you LORD JESUS!

OTHER BOOKS BY
Apostle John Devries

"Fivefold Foundation Ministries: Connecting Locally, Reaching Globally," *Fivefold Foundations Ministries Inc.*, **http://www.fivefoldmin-istrychurches.com**

Fivefold Churches Doctrinal Manual (forty-two study topics on needed doctrinal truths)

Apostle's Fivefold Doctrine Manual (nine study topics on basic foundational truths)

Salvation Gained and Maintained with Holy Fear Manual (five study topics that all believers should know)

A Christ Appointed Ministry: The Call of God. Lake Mary, FL: Charisma Media, 2012 (a book defining the real call of God to ministry)

Fivefold Churches (a book detailing Christ's multiple callings, eldership, accountability)

Christian Divorce and Remarriage: A Scriptural Exposition. Mustang, OK: Tate Publishing and Enterprises, 2011 (a book setting out scriptural doctrine of Christian divorce and remarriage)

Recommended resources:

Beck, Apostle Pete Jr. *Not Many Fathers*. Knoxville, TN: Master Press, 2013.

Dr. Kevin Orieux, church and believer finances with blessings teaching (You can contact him through his company, Aararat Consulting, at **www.aararat.com**)

Ray, Jasper James. *God Wrote Only One Bible*. Eugene, OR: Eye Opener Publishers, 1984.